David Hansen and The Call to Teach

Renewing the Work That Teachers Do

EDITED BY

Darryl M. De Marzio

TEACHERS COLLEGE PRESS

TEACHERS COLLEGE | COLUMBIA UNIVERSITY
NEW YORK AND LONDON

Published by Teachers College Press,® 1234 Amsterdam Avenue, New York, NY 10027

Cover credit: Winslow Homer (c. 1870). *The School Mistress*, [Oil on canvas]. Gift of Dr. and Mrs. Roger Kinnicutt. Worcester Art Museum, Worcester, MA.

Library of Congress Cataloging-in-Publication Data

Names: De Marzio, Darryl M., editor.
Title: David Hansen and the call to teach : renewing the work that teachers do / edited by Darryl M. De Marzio.
Description: New York, NY : Teachers College Press, [2021] | Includes bibliographical references and index.
Identifiers: LCCN 2020033050 (print) | LCCN 2020033051 (ebook) | ISBN 9780807764565 (paperback) | ISBN 9780807764572 (hardcover) | ISBN 9780807779187 (ebook)
Subjects: LCSH: Teaching—Vocational guidance. | Teaching—Philosophy. | Hansen, David T., 1962– The call to teach. | Hansen, David T., 1962– —Influence.
Classification: LCC LB1775 .D255 2020 (print) | LCC LB1775 (ebook) | DDC 371.1—dc23
LC record available at https://lccn.loc.gov/2020033050
LC ebook record available at https://lccn.loc.gov/2020033051

ISBN 978-0-8077-6456-5 (paper)
ISBN 978-0-8077-6457-2 (hardcover)
ISBN 978-0-8077-7918-7 (ebook)

Printed on acid-free paper
Manufactured in the United States of America

For teachers everywhere who heeded the call
during the COVID-19 pandemic

Contents

Acknowledgments

I owe several colleagues and friends thanks for helping to bring this book along the way from concept to publication.

Megan Laverty was the first to hear my idea for the book and offered encouragement and invaluable advice. Perhaps her best suggestion was that Teachers College Press was the natural home for this project. I am extremely grateful to Brian Ellerbeck and the outstanding editorial team at TC Press for their patience, guidance, and support throughout.

I am very fortunate to have several colleagues at the University of Scranton who have generously given their time to discuss with me the craft of teaching (often in vocational terms). I want to thank Maria Oreshkina, Tata Mbugua, and Jennifer Kaschak of the Education Department; Nathan Lefler, Charles Pinches, and Patrick Clark of the Theology Department; and Duane Armitage, Patrick Tully, and David Black of the Philosophy Department. Working with such committed professors is a daily reminder of just how vital the sense of vocation remains to the practice.

I first read *The Call to Teach* under the best possible circumstances—as a doctoral student in the Philosophy and Education program at Teachers College, Columbia University. The program was then, as it remains today, a remarkable place of learning. I am grateful to the many friends, colleagues, and professors who have nourished the intellectual soil of that venerable institution throughout the years.

For the past 12 years, David Hansen has graciously invited me back to New York City in the summer months to teach a course titled "The Call to Teach." This has afforded me the opportunity to reread and critically discuss selections of Hansen's work with hundreds of master's- and doctoral-level students. Those interactions have been instrumental in bringing this book to the light of day.

Most importantly, I am forever grateful to my wife, Anne Cecilia De Marzio, and my wondrous children, Dino James, Iris Annie, and Romola Catherine. The finishing edits of this book were completed during the spring of 2020, while we all sheltered in place because of the coronavirus outbreak. Their patience, love, and understanding helped make this book possible.

CHAPTER 1

The Language of Vocation and the Prospect for Teacher Renewal

An Introductory Essay

Darryl M. De Marzio

This collection of essays on the work of David Hansen is motivated by a desire to *retrieve* and to *renew* the sense of vocation in teaching. In special recognition of the 25th anniversary of the publication of Hansen's first book, *The Call to Teach* (1995), the authors of the chapters that follow consider it an essential task that we return to the language of vocation in teaching—a language developed by Hansen, not only in *The Call to Teach* but in subsequent writings throughout his distinguished career. These essays are therefore a testament to that career—to a career dedicated to teaching and scholarship, and to a legacy of profound influence on teachers, teacher educators, philosophers of education, and educational researchers the world over. Furthermore, these essays are also a testament to the prospect of teaching, a prospect that appears all the more crucial as the world hurtles headlong into the 21st century.

THE CRISIS IN TEACHING

Teaching today, much like it was 25 years ago, is in a state of crisis. Teachers continue to face mounting scrutiny from all corners over the efficacy of their practice. The public demand for greater accountability of teachers, particularly in the United States, has led to policies that place ever more emphasis on standardized measures of assessment of student learning and teacher performance. Some observers note that the increasing fixation on quantitative metrics for the evaluation of teaching, such as standardized student test scores, has profoundly degraded the value and meaning of the work, resulting in teachers fleeing the profession at staggering rates (Muller, 2018). These observations are buttressed by surveys of teachers that report the main reason they give for leaving the profession—even beyond financial considerations—is an overall feeling of dissatisfaction with the job.

Furthermore, the driving factor for such general dissatisfaction is most often associated with displeasure at the recent intensification of assessment and accountability measures (Sutcher et al., 2016).

The overall malaise felt by many who have taught or currently teach in schools seems also to have trickled down to the next generation of prospective teachers. Across the United States, for instance, college and university teacher education programs have witnessed severe declines in enrollment over the past decade, where more than one-third fewer students now major in teaching than in 2010 (Partelow, 2019). This hardly comes as a surprise, especially when we consider that the generation of students who are now entering college and university have mainly seen the practice of teaching through a lens crafted by such policy strictures as No Child Left Behind. Still, the crisis of declining enrollment in teacher education programs, and of teacher shortages generally, is not a problem unique to the United States. The global aim of providing every child with an equitable primary and secondary education necessitates that the demand for teachers in the near future far outpace the current global recruitment levels (Ingersoll et al., 2018). If the degree of dissatisfaction expressed by the current crop of schoolteachers continues, and fewer people enter the ranks, it is more than likely that a large share of the world's student population in the coming years will be educated virtually or with the assistance of robotic teachers (Edwards & Cheok, 2018).

While the challenges described above may be unique to today's teaching workforce, they bespeak the sorts of struggles that past generations of teachers have also faced. In short, the public pressure and personal malaise felt by today's teachers, much like the problems faced by their counterparts in years past, all relate back to the need for teachers to experience their craft in vocational terms. In other words, teachers continue to need teaching to be recognized by their students and the public at large as a worthwhile endeavor. But teachers also need for the practice itself to offer opportunities for personal meaning and fulfillment. As Hansen put the matter 25 years ago, "analogues to [these] contemporary pressures have always accompanied teaching in schools. . . . In short, the shape and terms of the difficulties facing teachers may have changed, but not the inherent challenges themselves" (Hansen, 1995, p. 133). This book, therefore, is the collective effort not just to retrieve ideas that Hansen may have articulated in the past, but to bring those ideas to bear on the unique challenges today's teachers face in order to renew the work that teachers do.

THE LANGUAGE OF VOCATION IN TEACHING

Why vocation now? As the Hansen quotation cited above suggests, the prospect of teaching today poses many challenges that have long been characteristic of the practice. Some of those challenges have to do with what goes on *within* teaching—that is to say, with the sorts of struggles teachers themselves confront and perceive in the work. Some of the challenges, however, have more to do with the perspective of teaching held by those *outside* the practice—by parents and students certainly, but also researchers and policymakers. In both cases, much will depend on the terms employed to describe teaching. The language of teaching informs and shapes our understanding of teaching, of how we judge and perceive the practice, whether inside or outside of it. It is in this sense of employing a certain kind of language with regard to teaching—*a language of vocation*—that Hansen develops the concept of vocation in teaching. The first step in a project of renewing teaching, therefore, is to reconsider the terms of teaching, to think again about the language that we use to describe this distinctive and time-honored human activity. To ask "Why vocation now?" is essentially to ask, "Why use the language of vocation to describe teaching?"

For Hansen, using the language of vocation does not promise to yield a complete understanding of teaching, as if the term itself were a Platonic category capable of capturing teaching with permanency. The very complexity of the work, and the fluidity of circumstances in which teaching happens, makes such absolute knowledge, regardless of the terms we employ, impossible. Instead, the language of vocation allows for certain dynamic features of the practice to emerge, features that tend to be shielded from view when other notions to describe teaching are employed. Such features, in a word, involve the *centrality of the person* who occupies the role of teaching. This notion—that the person who teaches is of foremost importance when it comes to describing, understanding, and evaluating the practice—is perhaps the major theme, and the major outcome, of Hansen's study of teaching as a vocation. It is a theme that I touch more on in the section that follows. It is therefore to Hansen's great credit to have observed that the more customary descriptors of teaching used in public discourse, as well as in much educational research, fail to appreciate the personal dimensions at stake in teaching. Terms such as *job, profession, occupation*, and *career* tend to treat teaching as an activity performed by a replaceable functionary. Such language "leaves completely out of the picture the human being who performs the activity" (Hansen, 1995, p. 8).

Naturally, the language we use to describe teaching will inevitably frame the manner in which we conduct research on teaching. References to teaching in occupational terms, such as a *career, job, profession*, and the like, are prevalent in sociology and political science because such terms allow those domains of inquiry to understand teaching in the context of large, bureaucratic structures. Similarly, research in psychology employs these exact terms to describe teaching broadly in order to determine phenomena such as career choice patterns. As Hansen puts it, "These lines of research have provided language and perspectives for thinking about teaching as a job and as an occupation nested within a broader system of social institutions" (Hansen,

1994, p. 260). Within these research disciplines, therefore, the personal dimensions of teaching tend to fade from view. Offering a language of vocation in teaching thus aims to fill in this missing picture within educational research. In this way, *The Call to Teach* not only provides a philosophical diagnosis of this lacuna in research on teaching, but presents an instance of empirical educational research that takes seriously the person who occupies the role. The book is therefore an exemplary and early instantiation of an emerging approach to doing educational research that blends philosophical analysis with empirical methodologies (Wilson & Santoro, 2015).

Employing the language of vocation in teaching, however, is not simply a matter of calling teaching a vocation as opposed to other, more commonly used labels. No matter how important such a change of vocabulary might be to our understanding of teaching, the language of vocation refers instead to a whole host of ways in which teachers and scholars describe the practice in terms that reflect the personal meaning teaching offers teachers, as well as the social value it upholds. When it is conceived as a vocation, we understand teaching to offer its practitioners "a sense of self, of personal identity" and "personal fulfillment" (Hansen, 1995, p. 3). Importantly, however, Hansen is keen to note that the practice offers practitioners various sources from which to derive personal meaning precisely through the ways in which teaching offers opportunities for teachers to give of themselves:

> [Teachers] bring into play in their work their knowledge of subject matter, of pedagogy, and of human development. They repeatedly make intellectual and moral judgments of their students' effort and conduct. . . . The personal fulfillment they derive from teaching may be a direct consequence of the very fact that they do bring so much of themselves to bear while on the job. (Hansen, 1995, p. 116)

To consider teaching as a vocation is therefore to consider the ways in which the social value derived from teaching overlaps with those areas in which the teacher derives personal fulfillment from the work. In this way, teaching is conceived of neither as a practice of pure selfless devotion, where greater social benefits accrue precisely to the extent to which the teacher renounces their quest for personal fulfillment, nor as just another market-driven profession, motivated purely by financial incentives and the promise of advancing up the career ladder. Instead, teaching as a vocation entails that in giving oneself over to the work, the teacher generates *both* social value and personal fulfillment.

From this perspective, *The Call to Teach* can be read as a philosophical meditation on the testimony of four teachers, from four unique school settings, who describe and embody their work in the language of vocation. This is not to suggest that it is a work of "pure" philosophical meditation, where Hansen's analytical voice dominates the scene. Nor is it to suggest that *The*

Call to Teach is the work of a neutral and disinterested observer, simply reporting on what these four teachers happen to say about their work, or on what their behaviors in the classroom suggest about teaching. As noted above, Hansen's book is a considered a blend of two approaches—of philosophical reflection and analysis, on the one hand, and an empirical method of thick description on the other (Geertz, 1973). Hansen's philosophical orientation is to allow the vocational dimensions of what these teachers say and do, of how they interact with students and colleagues, and of how they structure their classrooms and lessons to emerge. He offers philosophical categories for thinking about teaching as a vocation by *showing* readers the personal meaning and social value in the work of these four teachers. These categories are what Hansen dubs the "senses of vocation" in teaching.

Hansen does not pretend to offer an exhaustive list of the senses of vocation in teaching, either in *The Call to Teach* or elsewhere. Instead, the senses of vocation are categories that emerge from the ground up, collected through observing the concrete, day-to-day happenings of the lives of actual teachers. They are what Hansen "bears witness" to when it comes to teaching (Hansen, 2017). Some of these senses include the teacher's manner of being an "architect" of their craft, rather than simply laboring in the work of teaching (Hansen, 1995, p. 116). Another sense includes "cultivating a sense of tradition" where teachers actively engage in conversation with the history of their practice (Hansen, 2001). One sense of vocation that Hansen frames in *The Call to Teach*, and that continues to fascinate him in subsequent writings, is the teacher's attention to detail. Hansen says that "discharging faithfully the often mundane chores that accompany teaching does not represent a distraction *from* the work. Rather, each of the seemingly minor acts and steps one takes adds up over time to the teacher one becomes and to the influence one might have on students" (Hansen, 1995, p. 117). What Hansen is referring to here is the drudgery of teaching, the quotidian demands that teachers in schools attend to: taking attendance, preparing materials, grading examinations, and so forth. Rather than having an aloof attitude toward these duties, and holding out their attention for activities seemingly more germane to teaching, such as lecturing or facilitating class discussions, teachers with a vocational orientation to the practice are mindful of the significance of even the most humdrum aspects of their craft. Furthermore, this sense of vocation develops over time. It becomes an important part of the vocational teacher's practice because being attentive to the details requires practice.

Hansen is by no means romanticizing the errands of teaching, or attributing a sentimental value to them. Instead, his work acknowledges that such practices are what helps give shape and form to the person who takes up the role. The manner in which teachers attend to the details reflects their intellectual and moral judgment, their conduct and attitude toward students and subject matter. In later works, Hansen (2011) relates this sense of vocation to those exercises of the self that both ancient and modern philosophical traditions saw as integral to the art of living. Teachers with such a sense of vocation, much like their philosophical counterparts, consider the details of the craft as constituting part of the personal meaning they derive from the practice: "They constitute a self-pedagogy, an ongoing process of *forming* oneself into the person and teacher one can become" (Hansen, 2011, p. 111).

In Hansen's writing, the language of vocation becomes a rich philosophical language. It helps us see features of the teaching life that wane when other, more conventional language to describe teaching is employed. The language of vocation draws our attention to the intellectual, moral, and aesthetic dimensions of the work precisely because it illuminates the ways in which teaching is very much a lived philosophy for the teachers who take up the practice. In other words, the language of vocation draws our attention to the person who occupies the role, and, further, to just how central to the role of teacher the person actually is.

THE CENTRALITY OF THE PERSON IN TEACHING

When once asked about teaching in the United States, the German philosopher Hans-Georg Gadamer told the following story: "Once I was teaching in Boston College and a student came to me and said, 'Oh, Professor Gadamer, I see that you are teaching Plato this semester! What a pity, because I have already done Plato!'" (Gadamer, 1992, p. 5). Gadamer's intention in sharing this anecdote was to make a point about the overregulation and bureaucratization of higher education—that once students get their fill of a certain subject they can proceed to something else, as if a course of study were akin to a consumable unit, to be disposed of once one was finished with it. I think, however, we can take Gadamer's story also as a parable of a misguided conception of teaching. Not only does the student miss the mark when it comes to understanding the significance of curriculum, but they also assume that *teaching Plato* amounts to the same thing for Professor Gadamer as it did for their previous professor. In other words, the student assumes that the person in the role of professor is interchangeable—that the person who teaches is more a function of the role, rather than the role of the teacher being a function of the person.

As I suggest above, the notion of the centrality of the person is perhaps the major upshot of Hansen's work on vocation in teaching. This notion acknowledges that when it comes to teaching, "Despite a host of common obligations and practices, no two teachers have the same personal and moral impact on students" (Hansen, 1995, p. 11). However, as Hansen readily admits, such a viewpoint does not mean that teachers are the sole authors of their practice. Teaching, much like other practices of longstanding tradition, occurs within and through a social medium. In this way, we can consider the individual teacher to be one who inhabits a role shaped and informed by teachers since time immemorial. It is not in spite of this fact that individual teachers offer their own personal stamp on the practice. Rather, it is precisely because of it. "Teachers would have no medium in which to work without the practice. Yet the practice would itself disappear without imaginative, active individuals to carry it forward into the next generation" (Hansen, p. 146).

Recognizing the influence of tradition or other social factors is not to deny the teacher agency altogether. It is instead to appreciate two factors: First, as Hansen puts it, "We do not know in any final sense how or to what extent individuals' beliefs, values, perceptions, and actions are shaped by their culture and society, nor, in contrast, to what extent they reflect their own unique dispositions and moral sensibilities" (Hansen, 1995, p. 129). All we can say with any degree of confidence regarding the person of the teacher and their relation to the practice as a social medium is that the individual teacher indeed contributes to the practice of teaching, but also that "[t]eaching makes the teacher" (Waller, 1932, p. 375). Such a view does not dodge taking a side on the question of what forms the teacher—whether the teacher is more a product of the conditions in which they work, or more influenced by their own personal characteristics. Instead, it is to acknowledge the profound complexity involved in the question of *who* the person is who teaches.

Second, recognizing the influences of tradition and social conditions on the teacher is to recognize the extent to which those influences operate on the individual teacher. Not in the sense of constructing the teacher so that they become merely the product of their social environment, but that it is precisely those influences that serve to *call* the person to the practice in the first place. In this way, the call to teach is not reducible to an interior, psychological phenomenon (Hansen, 1995, p. 5). It is not a quality gifted to the teacher by nature. A calling might be felt as an inner drive, or as a motivational impulse to act on the world in some way. However, the call to teach is best understood as "a set of impulses that are outward-looking and outward-moving, focused on what is calling one to act" (Hansen, p. 5). What calls the teacher to the work is therefore what the practice of teaching as a social medium offers—the pursuit of an intellectual discipline, the chance to engage one's moral and aesthetic judgment, to have lasting influence on the development of the young, or the flourishing of the old.

All these factors, and more, bring the person who teaches to the foreground of the practice. Teaching possesses a remarkable capacity for enlisting the many facets of what makes one human to the craft—one's beliefs and opinions, attitudes, sentiments, talents and interests, even one's doubts and uncertainties (Hansen, 1995, pp. 117–122). If teaching is a vocation that potentially offers this much to the person who teaches, then it becomes necessary to consider how best to prepare teachers for garnering personal meaning and fulfillment through the practice. On the one hand, teaching often will implicate the personhood of the teacher in ways that grip the teacher unawares. Narratives of novice teachers are often testaments to this phenomenon (Inchausti, 1993). Still, such narratives offer ample evidence that the teachers most likely to grow as persons within the practice are those who have a cultivated ear to first listen, and then respond, to the language of vocation embedded there. Such an ear or voice for the language of vocation in teaching requires an education—perhaps one provided by the mentoring of a more seasoned colleague, or perhaps from the experiences accumulated throughout one's life. Such instances seem far too prone to happenstance, however, to place much confidence in, which is why Hansen takes seriously the notion that formal teacher education programs ought to include humanistic study as part of teachers' beginning and ongoing development.

The proposal to enrich teacher education with humanistic study entails for Hansen the engagement with those global traditions of philosophy, both ancient and modern, whose inquiries concern such questions as "How to live well?," "How to orient oneself to others and to the world?," and "How to be a person in the world?" In other words, teacher education ought to incorporate the study of philosophy as the art of living. As I alluded to earlier, there are deep and abiding connections between the practice of teaching and philosophy as the art of living. Both share in exercises and practices whose aim is the development of the individual and the cultivation of the human prospect writ large. For the most part, however, the current study of philosophy in teacher education programs is justified because of its status as a foundational discipline. As one popular foundation of education textbook proclaims, "Philosophy, as applied to education, allows practitioners and prospective practitioners to apply systematic approaches to problem solving in schools and illuminates larger issues of the complex relationship of schools to the social order" (Sadovnik et al., 2017, p. 196). Seen in this light, the foundational justification for teachers' study of philosophy does little to address the vocational dimensions of the practice. Certainly such an approach has its place—teachers do well when they understand and apply the resources of humanistic and social science disciplines in order to perceive the relationship between their work in schools and the broader, complex issues that pertain to society. The problem, however, is that within this foundational horizon is a view of teaching absent of the vocational. In limiting philosophical study to the foundational, the centrality of the person in the role gives way to an overemphasis on the societal forces that shape and influence the practice. The contention here, however, is that philosophical study, as Hansen envisions it, will go a long way toward renewing the practice of teaching today.

RETURNING TO *THE CALL TO TEACH*

As in times past, many are concerned about the plight of teaching, but most of all are the teachers themselves. Large numbers of teachers the world over have become disconcerted by the recent intensification of scrutiny they face over their effectiveness. More and more, teachers consider themselves scapegoats for societal problems beyond their control (Public Agenda, 2003). The crisis of teaching today is therefore as much a problem of the devaluing of the ethos and spirit of the teacher's personhood as it is a problem of the depreciation of the tools in the teacher's toolkit. Retrieving a sense of vocation in teaching, and returning to the centrality of the person who teaches, is a crucial step toward reversing this decline in morale and encouraging teacher renewal. But why, specifically, return to David Hansen's work on the vocation of teaching? Why return to his writings, and specifically this occasion of the 25th anniversary of *The Call to Teach*, as a starting point for engaging in a project of teacher renewal?

Each of the authors in this collection have their own way of addressing these questions. Some do so more directly than others. For my part, and as a philosopher of education in particular, I believe that there are two important reasons for returning to Hansen, in addition to the ones I have already sketched in the pages above. The first reason has to do with the treatment of works in philosophy of education by the field. The field of philosophy of education tends to pull in either of two directions—on the one hand, most scholars in the field anchor themselves to the more canonical works of philosophers who have written on education. Here we need only to think of the countless articles and books that focus on the educational writings of the likes of Plato, Rousseau, and Dewey. On the other hand, there are those scholars in the field whose focus is more on philosophical issues and questions pertinent to education, and who draw from a wide range of sources and disciplines both within philosophy and beyond. None of this, in itself, is a bad thing. However, when attempting to map philosophy of education as a distinctive domain of inquiry, the borders and territories of that domain tend to become obscure. Only rarely do philosophers of education engage with other philosophers of education to discuss *their* work. This ongoing lack of mutual engagement has meant that many classic and important works written by philosophers of education over the last half-century, such as *The Call to Teach*, have not received the sustained treatment and consideration that they otherwise have warranted. This edited volume is an attempt to address that concern specifically with regard to *The Call to Teach*, but also to motivate others to take up the project of anchoring the philosophy of education to some of the major works written in the field over the last 50 years or so.

The second reason for returning to Hansen's work has to do with another gap in the field of philosophy of education. This gap concerns the divide between philosophers of education and those who work in schools and educational institutions (Arcilla, 2005). Many philosophers of education, like myself, teach and do scholarship within teacher education programs. We hope and believe that our work has a lasting influence on those who leave our classrooms and move on to teach and administer in schools throughout the world. However, for the most part, our relationship to the world of schools is limited. Far too many of us connect to this world only through our university classrooms, or through the off chance that a teacher or administrator, somewhere, has encountered our work when doing research. *The Call to Teach* remains both a reminder and a blueprint for how philosophers of education can step into the world of schools, and work to influence, but also learn from, the practitioners whom they encounter there. Hansen's career attests to the fact that philosophers and educators can speak fruitfully to each other.

There are several essays in this book that speak to Hansen's approach as a philosopher who inhabits places of learning, and who engages with teachers, in order to assay and develop ideas relevant to educational practice. In this respect, the articles by Catherine Bell, Caroline Heller, and Shelley Sherman are most to the point. Bell draws on her own experience of Hansen observing her 6th-grade class as part of his research on vocation in teaching. She focuses on how her subsequent study of John Dewey, on Hansen's recommendation, and in particular Dewey's idea of "interest," compelled her to pay closer attention to the moral content of her own classroom. Likewise, Heller also reflects on her longstanding collegial relationship with Hansen, and uses the writer W. G. Sebald as a means to draw connections to an important theme of Hansen's more recent work—the notion of "bearing witness" in educational inquiry. Sherman's chapter revisits Hansen's conception of vocation in teaching and focuses on how the language of vocation encourages teachers to inhabit the present moment with each student in their classrooms.

Along similar lines is the article by Margaret Macintyre Latta and her colleagues Elizabeth Saville, Lisa Marques, and Katie Wihak. The authors use four images of pedagogical method developed by Hansen in his second book, *The Moral Heart of Teaching*, to describe an inquiry-based classroom setting. The chapter stands out for its application of both empirical method and philosophical reflection.

A pair of articles in this collection consider Hansen's engagement with some of his main philosophical and literary interlocutors. Ruth Heilbronn's essay explores the several ways in which Hansen's ideas are influenced by his continuous engagement with John Dewey's philosophy. Indrani Bhattacharjee places Hansen in conversation with the Nobel Prize laureate Rabindranath Tagore, a figure Hansen engages deeply in his later book *The Teacher and the World*.

Other articles focus instead on major philosophical themes in Hansen's work. Pádraig Hogan discusses the significance of Hansen's notion of cultivating a sense of tradition in teaching. Anna Pagès considers how Hansen anticipates the philosophical question of the voice in *The Call to Teach*, and demonstrates how Hansen recovers the voice as a philosophical concept in his depiction of the lives of teachers in that work. Hansjörg Hohr explores the uniquely aesthetic dimensions of Hansen's philosophy of teaching, paying close attention to the metaphor of the teacher as artist and as practitioner of the art of living. Finally, Huajun Zhang shows how Hansen's work challenges conventional notions of education that divide teaching and learning into separate practices, whereas Hansen seeks to overcome this divide by establishing a sense of reciprocity between the two. Zhang then considers the ways in which Hansen's orientation to education can be located in some of the emerging trends in Chinese education.

While all the articles in this volume share a common interest in Hansen's work, each article can also stand on its own for its uniqueness, in terms of both points of emphasis and points of departure. This feature of the book is a testament to the diversity of its contributors—a group of scholars and educators representing eight different countries and several different academic disciplines. Taken together, the chapters will offer readers the chance to behold the breadth and depth of Hansen's work, as well as the vast reach of his influence on education and the practice of teaching.

REFERENCES

Arcilla, R. V. (2002). Why aren't philosophers and educators speaking to each other? *Educational Theory, 52*(1), 1–11.

Edwards, B. I., & Cheok, A. D. (2018). Why not robot teachers: Artificial intelligence for addressing teacher shortage. *Applied Artificial Intelligence, 32*(4), 345–360.

Gadamer, H.-G. (1992). Interview: The German university and German politics. The case of Heidegger. In D. Misgeld & G. Nicholson (Eds.), *Hans-Georg Gadamer on education, poetry, and history: Applied hermeneutics*. State University of New York Press.

Geertz, C. (1973). *The interpretation of cultures*. Basic Books.

Habermas, J. (1984). *The theory of communicative action: Reason and the rationalization of society* (T. McCarthy, Trans.). Polity Press.

Hansen, D. T. (1994). Teaching and the sense of vocation. *Educational Theory, 44*(3), 259–275.

Hansen, D. T. (1995). *The call to teach*. Teachers College Press.

Hansen, D. T. (2001). *Exploring the moral heart of teaching: Toward a teacher's creed*. Teachers College Press.

Hansen, D. T. (2017). Among school teachers: Bearing witness as an orientation in educational inquiry. *Educational Theory, 67*(1), 9–30.

Inchausti, R. (1993). *Spitwad sutras: Classroom teaching as sublime vocation*. Bergin & Garvey.

Ingersoll, M., Hirschkorn, M., Landine, J., & Sears, A. (2018). Recruiting international educators in a global teacher shortage: Research for practice. *The International Schools Journal, 37*(2), 92–102.

Muller, J. Z. (2018). *The tyranny of metrics*. Princeton University Press.

Partelow, L. (2019). What to make of declining enrollment in teacher preparation programs. Center for American Progress.

Public Agenda (2003). Stand by me: What teachers really think about unions, merit pay and other professional matters. Public Agenda.

Sadovnik, A. R., Cookson Jr., P. W., Semel, S. F., & Coughlan, R. W. (2017). *Exploring education: An introduction to the foundations of education*. Routledge.

Sutcher, L., Darling-Hammond, L., & Carver-Thomas, D. (2016). *A coming crisis in teaching? Teacher supply, demand, and shortages in the U.S.* Learning Policy Institute.

Waller, W. (1932). *The sociology of teaching*. Russell & Russell.

Wilson, T. S., & Santoro, D. A. (2015). Philosophy pursued through empirical research: Introduction to the special issue. *Studies in Philosophy and Education, 34*(2), 115–124.

CHAPTER 2

Evolving Enactments of Personal Fulfillment and Service in Teaching

Shelley Sherman

Teachers' aspirations to sustain a sense of identity, pursue personal fulfillment, and provide public service are challenged 25 years after the publication of *The Call to Teach*. A cacophony of disrespectful voices and a proliferation of policies have discouraged and disillusioned many serious-minded teachers, with many struggling to resist becoming what Hansen describes as "functionaries carrying out the dictates of others" (Hansen, 1995, p. 120). Standardization, value-added accountability measures for teacher assessment, privatization, and the commodification of education all have contributed to a deflation in teacher morale (Connell, 2013; Kumashiro, 2012; Mora & Christianakis, 2011; Noddings, 2014). Nevertheless, in spite of a seemingly bleak scenario, time-honored moral and intellectual traditions of teaching continue to flourish.

Hansen's elucidation of teaching as a vocation resonates with committed teachers who embrace a conception of teaching as an intrinsically moral and intellectual endeavor (Hansen, 1999). They are called to teach for both altruistic purposes and self-fulfillment (cf. Higgins, 2011). "Vocation," says Hansen (1995), "describes work that is fulfilling and meaningful to the individual, such that it helps provide a sense of self, of personal identity." Furthermore, the work "results in service to others and personal satisfaction in the rendering of that service" (Hansen, p. 3). Hansen's conception of teaching as a calling endures for teachers whose commitment to teaching is steadfast regardless of challenges leading others to abandon it.

To be sure, teachers have lost control over certain elements of their practice, including curriculum and assessment. But in spite of this loss, they can, and many do, maintain autonomy over the most vital aspect of their work, their interactions with students. Countless teachers prepare students to live fulfilling lives and garner personal fulfillment for themselves, as well, by creating caring, compassionate, truthful classroom environments, responsive to the unique needs of individual students. A vision of teaching as a vocation as Hansen conceives it demands no less.

Teacher educators can support new teachers' aspirations that mirror the characteristics Hansen ascribes to teaching as a vocation by rebalancing the priorities of teacher preparation, honoring the normative aspects of teaching as much as the technical. Such a shift becomes possible when teacher educators look beyond their role as supervisors and evaluators, engaging with candidates in what Roderick and Berman (1984) refer to as "fellow traveler" relationships. Emerging from these relationships are evolving understandings about worthy teaching; prominent among them are both the moral and intellectual dimensions of the practice associated with responsiveness to students as complete human beings (cf. Sherman, 2013).

In one sense, teacher education programs do well preparing teachers for the realities of an educational landscape in which the protocol of teacher preparation echoes standardized K–12 curriculum. But teacher education programs are not courageously leading the charge to inform and reconstruct the public's understanding of what constitutes worthy educational endeavors, often narrowly confined to the pursuit of economic competitiveness and individual advancement, although they are in a singularly unique position to do so. In addition to equipping teacher candidates with the knowledge and skills needed for technical competency, teacher educators can cultivate dispositions for responsive teaching and elevate candidates' awareness of their responsibility to inform public understandings of educational purposes by examples of practice, beyond the actual, with an eye toward the possible. In my view, Hansen's notion of service as an enactment of vocation has rich potential in this regard, and I will return to it later in this essay.

Clearly, the challenges facing K–12 teachers and administrators are mirrored in teacher education. High-stakes performance-based assessments required for teacher certification have led teacher educators in the United States, for example, to teach to the test (cf. Greenblatt & O'Hara, 2015). In one self-study, teacher educators found themselves "teaching for compliance; [moving] from talking about teaching to talking about rubrics" (Cronenberg et al., 2016, p. 130). Images of teacher educators and candidates as fellow travelers in this regard are hardly inspirational, nor do they capture normative aspects of teaching embodied by its moral and intellectual dimensions. Teacher education is more about *performing* as a teacher than about *being* a teacher. Hansen elaborates on this difference time and time again as he explains how it is the person in the role of teacher whose importance transcends all other aspects of teaching, including teaching technique or curriculum (Hansen, 1998; 2001).

The person in the role of the teacher is crucial to Hansen's notion of teaching as a calling, pivoting around identity, personal fulfillment, and service, areas to which teacher preparation programs may pay only lip service. There is no formula to help candidates enact each facet of vocation described by Hansen, no mandated standards, no program to implement to satisfy accreditation. What is required, however, is a sufficiently generous space within the realm of teacher education in which each person's unique vision of enacting vocation begins to take shape within its own particular contours. By nurturing the seeds of this vision, teacher educators provide a foundation for lifelong commitment to the practice even as conditions in the field change over time.

Do conditions today make it more difficult for teachers to achieve their aspirations than was possible in 1995? Hansen reminded us then that "[T]he shape and the terms of the difficulties facing teachers may have changed, but not the inherent challenges themselves" (Hansen, 1995, p. 133). He argued that contemporary pressures in 1995 were analogous to, and relatively no more challenging than, pressures 100 years earlier. Is this analogy a timeless one? Although space does not permit a thorough investigation of this question, recognition and understanding of the shape and terms of difficulties today go hand in hand with efforts to sustain teachers' aspirations to pursue personal fulfillment and serve others. I suggest here how teachers and teacher educators viewing their work as a vocation can respond to changes over time, without compromising their aspirations. They can envision evolving meanings of personal fulfillment and service by recognizing what is immediately in their control and what is not. Teachers can locate opportunities to actualize normative aspects of teaching and do so with tenacity, especially because these aspects of their practice are not subject to standardized measurements, are deeply consequential to the well-being and growth of their students, and remain fundamental to their personal fulfillment.

Hansen's prodigious scholarship over time inspires thinking about the nature of vocation within today's educational, political, and social environment and beckons us to situate explorations of identity, personal fulfillment, and service in innovative, meaningful ways within the heart of teacher education programs. In the sections below, I discuss three features Hansen associates with vocation: identity, personal fulfillment, and service. The intersections among them are, indisputably, numerous. I distinguish them solely for heuristic purposes, drawing from prominent themes across Hansen's scholarship, including the person in the role of teacher and the notion of attentiveness. An enactment of Hansen's conception of teaching as a vocation is a portrayal of teacher preparation as an inspirational practice (cf. Sherman, 2013), rather than as an instrumental one.

IDENTITY AS AN ENACTMENT OF VOCATION

Questions about what it means to be a person in the role of teacher, suggests Hansen (2018), "are not merely philosophers' questions but animate serious-minded teachers in diverse ways" (Hansen, p. 24). But finding the time and fortitude to delve into questions posed by philosophers is a difficult task for teachers already consumed by the daily demands of teaching and challenging for teacher educators who mentor them under countervailing conditions. As Hansen (1995) reminds us, "The moment one steps into public life, as all teachers [and teacher educators] do when they walk through the doors of their schools and classrooms, one enters an unpredictable world that will require compromise and adaptation" (Hansen, p. 160). The pursuit of meaning as a person in the role of teacher is an arduous task in the face of complex boots-on-the-ground conditions over which teachers have little control. While teachers may try to stay in close touch with their identity, personal values, and aspirations, they must exercise a singularity of purpose against considerable odds to do so. To this point, Hansen (2018) argues for the need to introduce new teachers to the notion of investing themselves as persons in the role and warns that attrition may result from not doing so.

Most teacher education programs offer no oasis in this regard. External accreditation mandates demand maximum attention to behavioral surface rather than to the values underlying it, values that render each person a unique individual in the role of teacher. A narrow lens on technical performance in classroom observations does not provide a wide enough vantage point to recognize and honor a teacher's words and actions as compelling representations of personal identity and values (cf. Hansen, 2018, p. 23). Consequently, the identity of the *person* in the role of teacher may remain hidden in plain sight. Nevertheless, we can draw inspiration for illuminating a teacher's personhood by considering Hansen's field-based inquiry (see, for example, Hansen, 1995; 2017; 2018) in which he investigates how the unique capacities and dispositions of teachers express themselves in the classroom. In doing so, he animates the idea of vocation in teaching "to underscore the centrality of who occupies the role . . ." (Hansen, 1995, p. 11). Hansen's field inquiry, including his most recent, which he frames as *bearing witness* (Hansen, 2017), suggests possibilities for teacher educators and candidates to engage in like-minded endeavors, encouraging them to pursue philosophical questions, which are not "merely philosophers' questions." In doing so, teacher educators can help each candidate value and express their identity as a person in the role of teacher, or as Hansen describes it, find themselves in the practice. Bearing witness, explains Hansen (2018), "shed[s] light on the *meaning* people ascribe to their thoughts and actions" (Hansen, p. 29).

Classroom contexts provide abundant opportunities to pursue such exploration. On first glance, classrooms are public spaces occupied by aggregate groups, as those walking casually down school hallways might observe. But they are constituted by the innumerable privately lived experiences of individual teachers and students. As a teacher educator, to be fully present in these spaces is to have the privilege of bearing witness to something decidedly personal from both students' and teachers' points of view. This privilege provides both an opportunity and a responsibility to redirect a predominantly technically aimed lens of classroom observations toward the normative qualities of teaching and learning that cannot be discerned just by looking, but by seeing (cf. Van Manen, 2002), not just by hearing, but by listening. Such redirection is consistent with that which is advocated by Garcia and Lewis (2014), who call for movement toward phenomenological curriculum development in teacher education, "open[ing] the possibility for revitalizing teaching against both intellectual abstraction and skillful instrumentalization" (Garcia & Lewis, p. 165). In my view, phenomenological curriculum in teacher education and bearing witness conjure images of teacher educators and candidates as "fellow travelers," who seek to dig below surface behaviors, understand the meaning of responses to students, and get closer to students as unique human beings with particular needs to whom teachers need to be responsive. What would this look like within the structure of traditional clinical experiences in teacher education? Here, I share a hypothetical scenario as an example of such an image:

> The school day starts and students are engaged in morning activities. The teacher candidate, Elizabeth, has provided directions for the first portion of the day, and she moves on to work with a small group of students when a student, Mario, enters, several minutes late. Elizabeth looks up and, without leaving her seat, tells Mario how pleased she is to see him; asks another student, Eli, to help Mario catch up with the class; and continues to work with the group.

A mundane event at first glance is saturated with meaning for both the student and the teacher, meaning that can be revealed with further investigation and dialogue between the teacher educator and teacher candidate: What was Elizabeth thinking when she welcomed Mario? Why did she ask Eli to assist him? Would she address the reasons for the tardiness? When and how? A teacher candidate may be surprised by the direction of such questions, not recognizing anything significant about her own words or actions and expecting a discussion about lesson goals, strategies, outcomes, and so forth. Elizabeth's values, represented by her words and actions, are made visible through the fellowship of teacher dialogue, highlighting choices she has made quickly during a fleeting moment: I am happy see you (versus why are you late?). I want to be sure you have what you need (versus figure it out yourself). We are a community (versus a group of individuals, each interested only in their own well-being). Elizabeth's responses communicate her personal connection with the student, pleasure with, and gratitude for, his presence. Furthermore, Elizabeth's request to Eli to assist Mario is deliberate. She has noticed Eli's difficulty collaborating with others. He is shy and reluctant to initiate interactions with classmates. She seeks to boost his confidence and provide opportunities for him to engage with classmates in simple, structured, unintimidating ways. In addition, Elizabeth is communicating to the group of children with whom she is working to be patient as they witness her interactions with Mario. Elizabeth's words and actions reveal who she is as a person in the role of teacher. They also indicate her attentiveness to the needs of students and her ability to be responsive to particular students at a particular moment in time. I say more about such responsiveness in the following section.

The conduct and words of teachers can communicate care, kindness, respect, patience, thoughtfulness, dignity, and an emphasis on communal responsibility, to name just a few underlying values; or they can convey exactly the opposite. Meaningful dialogue in teacher education inspired by authentic events renders explicit the unstated underlying values of the person in the role of teacher, although the teacher may not realize they are expressing and modeling those values repeatedly in subtle ways. By helping a candidate articulate values, teacher educators render these values visible even when a candidate does not recognize them or takes them for granted. As Hansen reminds us, individuals considering teaching "may indeed have something to offer that nobody else can provide—even if the person may not appreciate (as yet) what the 'something' might turn out to be" (Hansen, 1995, p. 11). Teacher educators can assist candidates in a process of self-exploration to discern more clearly, comprehend more deeply, and embrace and question more frequently (see Hansen, 2017, p. 13) the persons they are becoming as they pursue the work to which they have been called. Hansen anchors such self-exploration to his conception of vocation:

> A calling, or vocation, characterizes a line of endeavor that beckons ("calls") the person to it, saying, in effect, you will find your *self* in this work, just as it will "find itself," that is, come alive, in you. (Hansen, 2018, p. 40)

Elevating the role of dialogue in teacher education in this regard is crucial toward assisting teacher candidates in examining their identity as they immerse themselves in the practice of teaching. Classroom interactions not only reveal a great deal about a teacher's identity, they also provide opportunities for teachers to recognize the autonomy granted to them and lead them to understand the significant responsibility attached to it.

As every person in the role of a teacher can find themselves in the practice, so does every teacher experience personal fulfillment and joy in teaching in distinct ways. Although personal fulfillment is often cited as a primary motivation to teach, teacher education programs may not pay heed to the ways in which it manifests itself throughout the course of teacher preparation in clinical placements. This is understandable given the demands placed on candidates and programs to meet certification requirements. But it also is shortsighted. Teacher preparation offers opportunities to identify and celebrate sources of personal fulfillment and keep in view the motivations to teach in the first place.

PERSONAL FULFILLMENT AS AN ENACTMENT OF VOCATION

Personal fulfillment is represented in a multitude of ways for teachers. In a broad sense, many teachers would see responsiveness to students as a fulfilling aspect of their practice because it is an indication they are making a difference in the lives of students. Elsewhere, I have discussed useful reference points for responsiveness (Sherman, 2013). One such reference point is the student themselves, which can be closely associated with personal fulfillment as an enactment of vocation. How teachers interact with each student, with careful consideration of the student's unique dispositions, capacities, and personal qualities, while keeping in mind vital educational aims, is at the root of responsiveness.

The word *response* can denote an action, an answer, or a reaction with either negative or positive connotations. Responsiveness, however, has a quality of receptivity, suggesting the empathic communicative capacity of the responder to say, "I understand you. I know you. I am sensitive to your needs. I am paying attention." Responsiveness to students requires strong content knowledge, agility at implementing a range of instructional strategies, as well as ethical qualities, such as care, respect, and fairness; a desire to understand students as whole human beings; and an intention to make a positive difference in their lives. Close attentiveness enables teachers to understand students from several perspectives, informing interactions with particular students at particular moments in time. With attentiveness, teachers can recognize preferences of learning modalities, gain insight into social and emotional well-being, identify patterns of conduct, and discern habits of mind. Hansen (1999) suggests that both intellectual and moral attentiveness are situated at the heart of understanding students, distinguishing one from the other: "Intellectual attentiveness entails closeness to students' responses to subject matter. Moral attentiveness involves closeness to students' responses to opportunities to grow as persons" (Hansen, p. 183). Attentiveness to individual students in the manner Hansen describes guides responsive teachers in their interactions by pointing them toward the direction in which educational experiences should proceed.

Attentiveness also enables teachers to be responsive in wholly autonomous and personal ways, guided by their understanding of students, as well as by educational aims writ large. Since responsiveness defies certainty and invites interpretation, options for teachers to respond to students are numerous; choosing among them demands close attention to the student, as well as the insight, intellect, and moral sensibility to respond well. Furthermore, although teachers' autonomous decisions can have a positive impact on students, they also can be damaging when a teacher lacks an understanding of a student's social, emotional, and academic strengths and the personal disposition to be responsive to them.

Teacher education programs allocate a great deal of time to technical skills required for responsiveness, but many may not focus sufficiently on what attentiveness looks like in everyday interactions with students. I suggested earlier that the most vital area of practice over which teachers retain autonomy is their interactions with students. These interactions, when pedagogically powerful and relationally meaningful, are aspects of teaching that, for many teachers, reside at the heart of personal fulfillment in teaching. But interactions with students cannot be as pedagogically powerful or relationally meaningful absent keen attention to the student.

Teacher educators can cultivate a disposition for attentiveness as they work with candidates in clinical settings, making it more likely they are learning how to be responsive to students. Attentiveness leads to responsiveness at any particular moment by taking into account a teacher's understanding of the student, not just of the content. Here is a hypothetical example. A word of encouragement to Daniel when he struggles to express an idea in a writing assignment may be quite different from one to Miriam, even if the assignment is the same. Daniel's teacher has paid attention to how he is learning to work through writing challenges independently and wants to encourage him to use strategies the teacher has astutely observed. "Remember what you did last week when you hit a snag developing your narrative?" Daniel nods and starts writing again. The teacher moves on to Miriam, discouraged, her head on her desk. One sentence is legible on the page with several lines scratched out. "Let's look at what you have written so far. That actually reminds me about what you told me last week about your art class. How can you expand your first sentence to talk about that?" A teacher's words and tone convey a great deal. "I listened to you. I value who you are and what you have to say." Miriam's teacher is coming to know who she is as a whole person, not only as a student. Knowing what to say or do with a student at a particular moment requires knowledge far beyond that attached to a skill or content area. The person in the role of teacher comes to know the person in the role of student.

A responsive teacher pays close attention, enters the student's learning space, identifies the student's instructional point of need, and responds to it in respectful, purposeful ways. Teachers who are responsive use attentiveness to drive students' imagination and inspire their creativity; they recognize actualities and envision possibilities for every student, no matter their current situation. Many new teachers require assistance to develop the capacity for attentiveness.

Formal curriculum standards suggest the need for attentiveness and responsiveness to help students achieve measurable learning outcomes. The kind of attentiveness and responsiveness I speak of accomplishes this, too, but also results in incremental changes, building habits of mind such as perseverance, curiosity, resilience, and self-confidence, qualities visible to the discerning teacher and critical to student growth. Responsiveness in this sense represents a way of *being* with students that privileges the immediate moment with a student above all else, while keeping an eye on the direction of the student's future (Hansen, 1995). It encompasses all facets of teaching, including advancing academic skills, enhancing social–emotional development, and cultivating dispositions for living a full life.

It may seem too tall an order for teachers to come to understand students and be responsive in the ways I describe here. After all, teachers do not teach individual students all day long and do not have the luxury to attend to individual students, at will, in a tutorial-like fashion. The examples I use are intended to point to ways of interacting with students during the course of school days over time. No teacher can connect with every student every day with an intentional focus that yields understanding and enables the teacher to be responsive. But there are students with whom teachers never or rarely connect in the manner I describe. Days, weeks, months may pass before a meaningful individual encounter between a teacher and a particular student occurs. Responsive teachers ask questions such as these: When did I last speak to Alice? When did I last make eye-to-eye contact with Michael? There can be a tendency to either focus on or ignore the habitually silent, academically gifted, emotionally troubled, or behaviorally disruptive student. Teachers can move toward the responsiveness I describe by reflecting on how to increase opportunities for individual interactions with all students. Teacher educators can help candidates reconstruct lessons and organize time and space in classrooms to accomplish this. Small-group collaboration, student partnership projects, and an allotment of time for individual meetings with teachers afford opportunities to do so. Highly responsive teachers create structures in their classes to engage in dialogue with students in small groups or on an individual basis. They provide meaningful, specific feedback on written assignments, rather than repeated short generic remarks such as "well done," "good job," or "need to say more." Responsiveness in teaching is physically and emotionally demanding, time intensive, and requires diligent commitment to reflective consideration of individual students. These are conditions that teachers who see teaching as a calling accept as the necessary terms of the practice.

For the most part, teachers are not *either* responsive *or* not responsive. They may be, at different times, one or the other, or *mostly* one or the other. A teacher may be consciously working to become more responsive in incremental ways or more or less oblivious to opportunities or responsibilities in this regard. The role of teacher educators is to heighten this consciousness. Neither learning how to be attentive nor understanding how to be responsive can be programmed into teacher education curriculum on a linear step-by-step basis. But the pivotal role of attentiveness and responsiveness can be infused in every aspect of teacher education, especially within clinical settings. A teacher educator and candidate, as fellow travelers, engaged in dialogue, even about a single interaction with a student, can lead to an epiphany for a candidate who is on the cusp of recognizing how the power of responsiveness makes a difference in a student's life as well as their own. Responsiveness not only represents a moral intention to make a difference in students' lives; it also signals initiative, determination, and the intellectual capacity to transform moral intention into purposeful action.

SERVICE AS AN ENACTMENT OF VOCATION

Expressions of personal identity and personal fulfillment as enactments of vocation may transform the life of the teacher from functionary to a person with autonomous moral agency in the classroom. Can such autonomy also be associated with notions of service? Should it be? If not, is there a conception of service to which all teachers should commit themselves? If so, what would it entail? These questions and others invite serious dialogue among practicing teachers, teacher educators, and teacher candidates about the nature of service and fidelity to it. My intention in posing them is to stimulate larger conversations about the nature of service in teaching, how it can be conceptualized, how it can be actualized, how it can evolve, and how it is driven by context. Like most questions related to educational value, there are rarely formulaic answers.

Teachers, unlike physicians, members of Congress, or police officers, do not take a formal oath of service. Such oaths dictate how and how not individuals should conduct themselves in their professional lives in general terms, guiding them in the specifics of their daily work. For instance, members of Congress swear to uphold the Constitution, and physicians vow to remember they are treating sick patients, not diseases. We come to expect these individuals to uphold their pledge and are disappointed when they don't. Politicians are answerable to the citizens who elect them, and doctors are accountable to their patients. We have options to elect new political representatives, and, in some cases, have opportunities to choose a physician. But although students occasionally can choose to go to a certain school, they rarely can choose their teachers. All deserve a commitment to high standards of service. And although we hope all teachers serve for the betterment of students, there are teachers who do not serve their students' best interests. Teacher educators who do not recognize the difference among candidates in this regard place the education of countless students at risk.

The ways in which teachers serve students by virtue of their identity and as a function of their responsiveness to them as individuals are implicit representations of service to each one's academic, social, and emotional growth in particular ways. Teachers also serve school communities, their school boards, and parents. But earnestly committed teachers do not confine themselves to the terms of service established by others. Are there even broader implications of a notion of service? Hansen (1995) suggests that although new teachers bring hopes to "'remake the world' . . . the greatest influence a teacher can have is right under his or her nose . . ." (Hansen, p. 135). Arguments to the contrary would be difficult to support. But even if we wholeheartedly embrace this proposition, we can, simultaneously, look beyond it.

If we consider an enactment of vocation to be one with evolving meanings, we cannot disregard the changing shape and terms of contemporary society. Shouldn't students be assured that, no matter who teaches them, every teacher has pledged to serve their students by readying them for the terms and conditions of the society into which they have been born? Societal changes today are neither less rapid nor less significant than the societal changes Dewey (1990) discusses in *The School and Society*. "Those [changes] I shall mention," says Dewey, "are writ so large that he who runs may read" (Dewey, p. 8). Today, technology and social media have altered the character of personal human communication, for better and for worse. The world is not a more humane, safer, or environmentally cleaner place than it was when Hansen published *The Call to Teach*. It is decidedly less so in every respect. Public discourse is vitriolic and the cultural divide acute. And yet the potential to address the conditions of today's society are boundless. Protecting the Earth, generating productive civil discourse within and across political boundaries, and honoring the value of respectful, caring human relationships are substantively one and the same with broad worthy educational aims.

I have argued that the conditions of standardization and the commodification of education can inspire teachers to embrace the ways in which they retain autonomy in their interactions with students in classrooms. Similarly, the conditions of the world can strengthen teachers' resolve to create classroom environments that are sanctuaries of care, kindness, and thoughtful, respectful dialogue. Teachers can create learning environments saturated with aspirations toward making the world a better and more just place, socially, environmentally, and economically. Such environments are microcosms of an aspirational society in which individuals listen to, and speak with, another with great courtesy, respect, and empathy. These are places in which the tone teachers establish (cf. Van Manen, 1986) is one of calm thoughtfulness versus careless reaction. If teachers were to take an oath of service, it seems reasonable to suggest it would include a commitment to practice teaching in the manner I have characterized.

What role do teacher educators play as fellow travelers with candidates in constructing notions of vocation that include service both to each student and to society, writ large. Teachers have the potential to improve the lives of students, one at a time in their individual interactions with them and through the purposeful creation of caring, ethical, educative learning communities in which students can thrive. The experiences of students in classrooms, including what they learn and how they learn it and the person in the role of teacher, do or do not promote what Noddings calls the "nurturance of [such an] ethical ideal" (1984, p. 6). Although Hansen suggests that the greatest influence a teacher can have is right under their nose, the influence of teachers, he avers, extends far beyond the individual student. Hansen places the teacher at the center of what he calls a "web of connections" constituted by strands tying students to one another and to people outside of the classroom, as well. As we have seen throughout history, a single individual can have an extraordinarily positive impact or a horrifically devastating one on countless other human beings. In this sense, worthy teachers provide service that can yield inestimable social value.

Profound educational values, to which Hansen often refers, may be reinvigorated when envisioning an evolving meaning of service as a touchstone for teacher preparation.

If these are aims with which we would be hard-pressed to disagree, what are the implications for teaching and teacher preparation in the context of a competitive, quantitatively measured, relatively normative-avoiding educational environment? What components of worthy teaching support such an endeavor? How can teachers embrace the notion of service in a way that promotes human flourishing and captures a collective sense of service as it represents the notion of teaching as a calling? These vital questions demand the concentrated attention of teacher educators today.

A FINAL WORD

When I began doctoral studies with David Hansen, close in time to the publication of *A Call to Teach*, I wondered aloud, when meeting with him in his office, how the philosophical work in which he was engaged was practically connected to the day-to-day, nitty-gritty work of teachers. David, not at all offended by my chutzpah and showing no disrespect for my naivete, patiently, and not at all defensively, began a dialogue with me that would continue throughout my doctoral program and beyond. I quickly came to understand how philosophical study, accompanied by field study, could be compellingly linked to the boots-on-the-ground practices of teachers, as well as to my own work as a teacher educator. His profound influence on me, and, by extension, on my own students, cannot be overestimated, and I am deeply indebted to him.

Shifting winds threaten to steer classroom teachers, teacher educators, and administrators off course (a truism both contemporaneous and historic), away from, rather than toward, the reasons they chose teaching. But today's particular challenges also operate as catalysts for like-minded educators to hold steady to aims that drew them to the practice in the first place, including the pursuit of personal fulfillment and service. Teachers and teacher educators, fueled by the energy and passion that called them to teaching, can breathe new life into the vocational aspirations of teachers to serve others and achieve personal fulfillment, helping them become more responsive to students, to themselves, and to society.

Students' hearts and minds can be nourished in schools with an aim toward walking the path of an honorable, principled life, owning dispositions that lead them to listen as much or more than they speak and care *for*, as much as they claim they care *about*, those in diminished circumstances. These dispositions include open-mindedness, compassion, humility, curiosity, resilience, and more. Although the development of such dispositions may be embedded, and even explicitly expressed, in curriculum standards, they must be modeled and practiced more consciously in schools. What's more, these capacities must be seriously valued—not just be paid lip service—by the public-at-large as central, legitimate educational goals.

Difficult questions emerge if we consider David Hansen's notion of teaching as a calling, not only as a vision by well-meaning prospective teachers, but also as a barometer to determine the worthiness of those entering the practice. Teachers may find self-fulfillment even when they are not making a positive difference in students' lives. Some who have little control of their lives outside the classroom may exercise it in ways detrimental to the cultivation and expression of democratic habits in the classroom. They may disregard broad aims of education, focusing on narrow personal agendas. As I mentioned earlier, autonomous decisions in the classroom may lead to better or worse consequences for students and communities alike.

This essay has focused on ways in which teacher educators can help sustain the vision of new teachers to fulfill aspirations to teach as an altruistic and personally fulfilling pursuit. A vitally important footnote to add is this: Dedicated teacher educators see teaching as a calling, too, for they are, first and foremost, teachers themselves. Elsewhere, I have written about teacher education as an inspirational practice (Sherman, 2013). Indeed, it can be, when teacher educators commit themselves to educate new teachers in a manner that embraces the practice as David Hansen conceives it. Teaching is, at one and the same time, habitually tiring, intellectually stimulating, emotionally draining, and personally fulfilling work. Accepting and meeting the entirety of its challenges head-on, with integrity and wholehearted determination, is not beyond the call of duty in the conventional sense of the phrase. Rather, it is an abiding duty to one's calling.

REFERENCES

Connell, R. (2013). The neoliberal cascade and education: An essay on the market agenda and its consequences. *Critical Studies in Education, 54*(2), 99–112.

Cronenberg, S., Harrison, D., Korson, S., Jones, A., Murray-Everett, N., Parrish, M., & Johnston-Parsons, M. (2016). Trouble with the edTPA: Lessons learned from a narrative self-study. *Journal of Inquiry & Action in Education, 8*(1), 109–134.

Dewey, J. (1990). *The school and society.* The University of Chicago Press. (Original work published 1900)

Garcia, J. A., & Lewis, T. E. (2014). Getting a grip on the classroom: From psychological to phenomenological curriculum development in teacher education programs. *Curriculum Inquiry, 44*(2), 141–168.

Greenblatt, D., & O'Hara, K. (2015). Buyer beware: Lessons learned from edTPA implementation in New York state. *Teacher Education Quarterly, 42*(2), 57–67.

Hansen, D. T. (1995). *The call to teach.* Teachers College Press.

Hansen, D. T. (1998). The importance of the person in the role of teacher. *Child and Social Work Journal, 15*(6), 391–405.

Hansen, D. T. (1999). Understanding students. *Journal of Curriculum and Supervision, 14*(2), 171–185.

Hansen, D. T. (2001). *Exploring the moral heart of teaching: Toward a teacher's creed.* Teachers College Press.

Hansen, D. T. (2017). Bearing witness to teaching and teachers. *Journal of Curriculum Studies, 49*(1), 7–23.

Hansen, D. T. (2018). Bearing witness to the fusion of person and role in teaching. *Journal of Aesthetic Education, 52*(4), 21–48.

Higgins, C. (2011). *The good life of teaching: An ethics of professional practice.* Wiley-Blackwell.

Kumashiro, K. (2012). *Bad teacher! How blaming teachers distorts the bigger picture.* Teachers College Press.

Mora, R., & Christianakis, M. (2011). Charter schools, market capitalism, and Obama's neo-liberal agenda. *Journal of Inquiry & Action in Education, 4*(1), 93–111.

Noddings, N. (1984). *Caring: A feminine approach to ethics and moral education.* University of California Press.

Noddings, N. (2014). High morale in a good cause. *Educational Leadership, 71*(5), 14–18.

Roderick, J., & Berman, L. (1984). Dialoguing about dialogue journals: Teachers as learners. *Language Arts, 61*(7), 686–692.

Sherman, S. (2013). *Teacher preparation as an inspirational practice: Building capacities for responsiveness.* Routledge.

Van Manen, M. (1986). *The tone of teaching.* Scholastic.

Van Manen, M. (2002). *The tact of teaching: The meaning of pedagogical thoughtfulness.* Althouse Press.

CHAPTER 3

Rising to the Needs of Pedagogical Situations

Method's Responsive Sensibilities and Responsibilities

Margaret Macintyre Latta, with Elizabeth Saville,
Lisa Marques, and Katie Wihak

INTRODUCTION

As a curriculum theorist and teacher educator, my scholarship and teaching attend to the aesthetics of human understanding—to its formative nature, asking all involved to adapt, change, and build meaning together. In doing so, I encourage educators to cocreate curricular experiences with their students, crossing disciplines and interests of all kinds. Rather than educators imposing predetermined teaching methods, the needed curricular responsiveness attending to given students, content, and context turns to a lived understanding of method as necessarily always in the making. Such an orientation to curriculum and teacher education builds on John Dewey's (1916) notion of how method is never independent of situation (Dewey, p. 165). Likewise, David Hansen (2001) also considers educators' sensibilities and responsibilities as emergent with contextual conditions and supports. Dewey (1910a) further insists that "actively to participate in the making of knowledge is the highest prerogative of man [sic] and the only warrant of his [sic] freedom" (Dewey, p. 127). Hansen's body of scholarship emphasizes the attentive roles educators assume in order to create such learning situations for knowledge, freeing meaning-making to occur. From this perspective, knowledge is understood as changing, contingent, and connected to the particulars of a situation, where deliberation and interaction are essential to the construction of knowledge. And curriculum is accordingly conceived as a continuous reconstructing movement of thinking. Hansen's scholarship offers rich language for attending to this reconstructing movement, as individual and collective sense-making take shape and

27

foster the learner/learning agency Dewey (1916) characterizes as freedom. Both Dewey and Hansen recognize the significance and potential of such participatory practice in education. They both envision how revolutionary knowledge-making can be, suggesting the powers and possibilities inherent within curriculum oriented toward growth, greater self-understanding, and enhanced well-being; curriculum that presents opportunities for teachers and learners to continually situate themselves meaningfully in the world. This chapter considers some of the rich learning ground that is encountered through curriculum-making. In doing so, the chapter reveals how such methodological terrain can in/form images of educational practice, mapping out the aesthetics of curricular enactment envisioned and brought to life through some of Hansen's key ideas, and shaping a lived language of Deweyan practice for all involved.

Dewey's (1916) declaration that participatory knowledge-making is central to being human, without resorting to the mere application of methods, strategies, and techniques alone, challenges educators to confront their basic understandings of knowledge, curriculum, and the roles of teachers, students, and context, within curricular enactment. Taking up this challenge in a combined grade 5/6 class with 60 students, three educators intentionally cocreate with their students, circumstances for active participation in the making of knowledge through science inquiry involving the study of water.[1] They seek within the concrete practice of knowledge-building discourses the needed responsive methodological terrain to do so. Turning to Hansen's (2001; 2005; 2011) language for knowledge-building brings to life Dewey's claim of method never being outside of materials (Dewey, p. 165) and illuminates this significance for all involved. It is a language that draws ongoing attention toward the learning context being created, and away from a teacher-centered focus. Furthermore, Hansen offers a language that fosters enlarged and deeper commitments toward knowledge-making discourses that take many shapes and suggest further learning directions across all disciplines and interests. Hansen (2001) refers to these as images of a growing person—guiding curricular attempts, steering deliberations, and cultivating confidence in process. Hansen characterizes such images as opportunities to "guide perception . . . assist(ing) the teacher to be alert to incipient signs of student agency and development. As teachers act on these signs, and learn from them, their image of a growing, educated person can broaden and deepen" (Hansen, p. 43). In what follows, four images of practice portray participating educators, alongside their students, embracing this pedagogical task. Dewey's (1916) unpacking of method as the "unity of subject matter and method," "method as general and particular"—both an art and adapted to exigencies, and revealing "traits of individual method"—serves as a guiding framework (pp. 164–179). Each image opens into possibilities for guiding, steering, and confidence-building, envisioning and reenvisioning curricular enactment within the given particularities of students, content, and context.

METHOD-IN-THE-MAKING

Image One: Unity of Subject Matter and Method

> In a large circle, 60 students are encouraged to share their recent biking and
> walking trips to local water resources—a pond, a lake, and a stream. They
> are asked to recall what they saw in the water, what they saw around the
> water's edge, and what they heard, smelled, and touched. These recollected
> journeys foreground the physical properties encountered alongside
> heightening awareness of plant and associated life within and near each
> body of water. The challenge for students is to identify coded water samples
> collected from each of these resources. These samples are accessible for
> further scrutiny and reference. The teacher shares some additional water
> samples she has brought with her from her family's hot tub, her son's
> aquarium, and the Okanagan Lake near her home. She invites students to
> ask questions about each of these water samples. What would they like
> to know? Lots of questions are generated including: Was the hot tub used
> regularly? Was the water temperature hot at time of sample-taking? Was
> the hot tub maintained regularly? Did the son clean the aquarium daily?
> What was the water temperature? How often were the fish fed? And how
> much food? What is in the aquarium as far as rocks, dirt, décor, etc.? How
> large is the aquarium? Are there fish and other life in the water? What is the
> land like around the section of the lake the sample came from? What animal
> and bird life are present there? What about plant life? Questions generate
> more questions and curiosity abounds regarding the extent of information
> that physical properties of water can reveal about each water source
> (Macintyre Latta, Field Notes, 2018).

The proximity of the biking and walking field trips alongside studying the
collected water samples provides much fodder for the students' recollected
accounts within the circle setting comprising Image One. The ensuing conversation brings much relevance to the students' study of water. As Dewey
(1916) explains, "method is a statement of the way the subject matter of
an experience develops most effectively and fruitfully" (p. 179). The teacher's sensibility to follow the development of the conversation draws students into relationships and furthers these relationships with water. Hansen
(2001) describes this sensibility as "straightforwardness," characterizing a
trust in students' reflective capacity to suggest ways to pursue the thinking
underway (Hansen, pp. 45–46). And, he articulates how teachers can seek
the conditions to elicit and support this movement of thinking in their students. In this image of practice, the teacher's attention to fostering a relevant
or invested connection for students is clear. Students come to care about
what each water source reveals through their direct contact, their questions,
and their continued ponderings. Even students who demonstrate little to

no interest initially in the inquiry discover questions they did not know they had through direct contact and their teacher's interest in their specific wonderings and connections. Straightforwardness manifests as a sensibility toward seeing and acting derived through what is heard, said, and felt—in other words, it is experienced as accessing the necessary curricular materials for knowledge-building discourses.

An individual/collective thinking movement is shaped as learners come together to pose questions, suggest theories, revisit, refine, and negotiate ideas. Creating the circumstances to facilitate such movement is interdependent with the discourses shaping the learning, embracing the learner/learning contingencies as the relevant risks and opportunities, and facilitating multidirectional dialogues invested in thinking. The internalized, enlarged, and deepened thinking that is generated characterizes the found unity of subject matter and method. As Hansen (2001) points out, it is teachers who must have intimate knowledge of such sensibility to ensure the needed trust in curricular situations, students, and self to pursue the needed conditions and supports. And teachers must concretely access how such sensibility liberates them from the assumption that method is something separate, "connected with the notion of the isolation of mind and self from the world of things," making instruction and learning formal, mechanical, and constrained (Dewey, 1916, p. 179). Hansen articulates such liberation as freeing teachers to embrace their "dynamic role" in supporting students to follow their thinking with found agency reorienting away from solely the task of teachers or solely the task of students, and toward the movement of individual/collective thinking, attending to the potential embodied within each moment as the movement of thinking unfolds (Hansen, pp. 45–46). The teachers involved in this image of practice organize the learning conditions and supports to optimize their dynamic roles. This includes attention to the external spaces to effectively support the ensuing thinking alongside attention to the internal time within the spaces to allow for immersive experiences. Fitting individual and collective paces for thinking are sought, unfolding in learning paths that students come to experience as straightforward—direction oriented, derived from encountered inner necessities, explicating Dewey's unification of subject matter and method.

Image Two: Method as General and as Individual—an Art

Following the opening circle conversation regarding the physical properties of particular water sources, students are arranged in groups of five or six at assigned tables. Situated around the circle meeting area, these tables each contain eight coded water samples, with the identification of each source purposefully masked. In table groupings, students begin to attend closely to the physical properties of each sample and make some warranted assertions about which water sample was particular to each water source. Group discussions consider the water's appearance, the materials floating in the water, the insects and larvae that were collected, and so forth. Tentative decisions are reached collectively and recorded on a data entry handout for each group. This process is seriously undertaken by students, and decisions are reached through some debate and much deliberation. Returning to large group circle conversation, students discuss their decisions to date, based on found and observed physical properties. New questions that surface include: Did students smell the water samples? What new or unexpected information did they use to reach decisions? These kinds of questions foreground the physical properties of water resources and initiate inquiry into chemical properties. A recent field trip to the local water treatment facility is recalled, bringing chemical properties into greater relevance. Large group conversation about the kinds of influences informing their judgments now include references to the surrounding land and to particular uses such as for orchards, farming, urban settings, pulp mills, and dairy animals. Conversations now turn to further reflective questioning regarding the surroundings of the collection sites of the respective bodies of water (Macintyre Latta, Field Notes, 2018).

The "unencumbered perception" Hansen (2001) describes as simple, spontaneous, naive, and required of teachers and, in turn, students is increasingly visible and tangible through Image Two. Hansen's depiction of the associated posture of focus and freedom of action is palatable (Hansen, p. 46). Students conduct small group conversations without guiding questions, without a worksheet offering linear instructions, and without a rubric outlining the key tenets to include. This unencumbered perception facilitates multidirectional conversations based on students' observations, connections, and recollections. The earlier large group conversation has clearly prepared students for such thought-provoking conversations. In small groups deciphering the various water samples, we observe students' intuitions surfacing and emotional responses informing decisionmaking. Teachers move in and out of these groupings, affirming and furthering this thinking as they deem fitting. Spontaneity occurs not as happenstance but as novel and arising out of the particularities of each group conversation. As students retrace their accounts, they take pride in their resulting unique approaches. Teachers honor the varied accounts and ensure all groups share their collective story of how thinking was stimulated. Naivete, understood as seeing again and again in new and varied ways, is concretely encountered as the smaller groups each share in the large group circle. Recursive learning opportunities are apparent as individual group members make connections to their thinking, evoked by the other groups.

Collectively, the conversation opens into new ideas and arising matters for continued consideration. The focus and freedom that animate Image are concomitantly a communally shared experience, one that acts as a catalyst for continued collective investment, while also empowering students on an individual basis. Fostering such focus and freedom of action insists on what Dewey (1916) terms teachers' artistry; an artful pedagogical method that is both general and individual, deeply knowledgeable about content and approaches to learning, while attending to given situations, students, and contexts. As each group reaches tentative decisions identifying the eight water sources, their commitment to their thinking and their capacities to articulate that thinking are striking.

Image Three: Method as General and as Individual—Adapted to Exigencies

New scientific terms are introduced by the teacher in reference to the water sources the students now have greater familiarity with and a growing commitment to learn more about. Each group is given an inquiry question that positions them to research further into the chemical properties of water including pH levels, nitrates, phosphorus, and chlorine ratios. For example, one of the groups researching phosphorus levels debates whether increased levels of phosphates indicate healthy or unhealthy biological systems. The group discovers that phosphates are an essential nutrient to support life, occurring naturally in all forms, both vegetable and animal. One student reads aloud from the research about how human genes, bones, teeth, and muscles all contain phosphates, a chemical compound present in the ecosystem long before humans arrived. Another student adds how phosphates form the raw materials for toothpaste, fertilizer, baking powder, evaporated milk, household cleaners, soft drinks, cured meats, water softeners, and many other products. A debate emerges as one student comments, "if it is an essential nutrient, that implies it is good," an indicator of a healthy system. But as two students point out, referring to the research they are examining, this is not always the case. These students discern that phosphates on their own are not bad. However, they note that local lakes in the Okanagan have been found in the past to contain abnormally high levels of phosphates. They paraphrase from the research findings, explaining how high levels are caused by runoff from agricultural fertilizers, domestic and industrial overuse of phosphate cleaners, and naturally high levels in our surrounding mountains. Another student exclaims, "It all comes down and accumulates in the lakes." Another student enters the conversation: "that is the problem." Collectively, students map out how the floating plants called algae, the smallest organism in the food chain, absorb the nutrient-enriched ("eutrophic") water and grow much too quickly in these conditions. As the algae dies, it uses up the oxygen in the water, literally smothering all other plant and marine life, and destroying the balance. So the chart they compose to document their findings about phosphorus levels and water quality attends to this debate and depicts everyday items containing phosphates, charting their emergent understandings of eutrophics.

All groups document on chart paper a collective understanding of the specific inquiry question particular to the given chemical property. Comparison tables, images, and statements are crafted. Large group circle sharing takes place, with each group asked to present their findings for others to learn and ask questions of each other. As each group shares their findings particular to each chemical, growing attention is oriented toward improved and upgraded sewage treatment plants, changes in agricultural practice (fruit trees giving way to vineyards) that need less irrigation and fewer fertilizers, and increase in public awareness for biodegradable products (Macintyre Latta, Field Notes, 2018).

"Openmindedness and openheartedness" are identified by Hansen (2001) as inquiry-oriented modes of being that need to be practiced in order to cultivate the habits that further participatory thinking. Hansen relays these modes as necessary, entailing an active receptivity (Hansen, pp. 51–52). And, indeed, within Image Three students find themselves actively confronting unfamiliar notions, attempting to make sense of them in relation to their individual and collective understandings. The research task by itself does not create the needed circumstances, rather it is the attention given to sense-making that cultivates an appreciation for the given diversities and histories brought to the particulars of each situation. Open-mindedness is reflected in students' willingness to change their minds as they turn their attention to deliberating the positive and negative implications of various pH levels. Openheartedness is reflected in students' embrace of the emotional commitment they bring to the sense-making process. And Image Three depicts how these modes work together, in Hansen's words, to "augment human connections and under-standing" (Hansen, p. 52). Dewey (1916) also reminds us of how such recep-tive modes authorize "the exigencies of particular cases" (Dewey, p. 171), as exemplified by the pH level group investigation that assayed specific needs, resources, difficulties, and values. Dewey's emphasis on "individual powers in activities that have meaning" (Dewey, p. 172) are affirmed throughout. Teachers are alert to doing so as they move between groups. Students respect each other's process in authoring their ideas and the directed action gener-ated, taking shape across each group. The robust and energized large group conversation continues to affirm these needed modes and habits. There is room for disagreement, room for struggle, room for speculation, and room for feelings of discomfort; in other words, method becomes general and indi-vidual, adapting to exigencies. "Roominess" (Dewey, 1934, p. 209) emerges via navigating individual and collective meaning-making processes that value open-mindedness and openheartedness.

Image Four: The Traits of Individual Method

Instructions for conducting one test—nitrate, phosphate, chlorine, or pH levels—are placed at each table grouping. Students are asked to return to their tables and carefully read the specific instructions and then to gather all necessary supplies and equipment for the experiment. As testing commences, students begin to document their findings. Much excitement and investment in carrying out the tests is observed. Information charts about what specific tests indicate are provided to table groupings to assist with sense-making. Data are compiled on a graph visible to all on a large whiteboard. Large group circle discussion provides an opportunity to share findings from each group and the chance to note revisions to previous judgments. Students are then charged with making a final assertion about the eight water samples given all the information collected regarding physical and chemical properties. Groups meet and seriously grapple with their final decisions, which are compiled for each grouping on a chart and placed in the middle of the circle for all to see. Students look for differences and similarities across all groups. Finally, the reveal of the origins of the coded water samples is announced. One group actually has all the water resources correctly identified. A team of five girls is bursting with pride. Most groups have about half of the water samples correctly determined. As students start to clean up and organize for departure, there is much talk of how this is the science they really like (Macintyre Latta, Field Notes, 2018).

The thinking movements underway as evidenced in Image Four speak to the individual/collective commitment that is mustered through attunement to the traits of distinct learning experiences. Students voice their varied decisions, tracing how each group reached them with much conviction. As Hansen (2001a) articulates, students find purpose, increasingly taking responsibility for the thinking underway, and approaching the undertaking with a serious-ness that permeates all groups and extends into continued learning opportunities and beyond to connections made outside of school. Such thinking reflects the attitude Dewey (1916) terms "intellectual hospitality" (Dewey, p. 175). Such an attitude fosters individual traits that guide efforts through respect for differences as potential mediums for sense-making. In this way, differences are valued for maintaining the vitality of present relations, and are an anticipated aspect of one's attunement to the learning process. Therefore, each group is able to take pride in their thinking with an accompanying at-titude of hospitality, appreciative of the distinct traits manifest across each group. Matters such as being right or wrong, finding the best solution, or be-ing first to arrive at an answer are not concerns that permeate the conclusion of this experience. Rather, a shared investment and accomplishment perme-ates the learning experience; and despite the weekend beckoning on a Friday afternoon, students linger to talk further with each other and their teachers about the water inquiry and how they envision further study.

TEACHING INDIRECTLY, SHAPING LEARNING CONTEXTS

The four images of practice explicated above vivify varying contributing fea-tures of Hansen's (2001) notion of "teaching indirectly" (Hansen, p. 61).

Hansen turns to Dewey's (1910b) unpacking of "readiness" understood as thoughtful consideration before reaching a decision, rather than dismissingly "passing judgement" (Dewey, p. 34), as central to the notion of teaching indirectly. It is through thoughtful and considered readiness that pedagogical situations become a methodological medium for opening the potential for teaching indirectly. Hansen characterizes this potential as "a posture of readiness to engage the world" (Hansen, p. 61). Image One calls attention to how the posture of readiness allows time and space to value thinking. Image Two reflects on how readiness allows for embracing the ongoing movement of individual and collective thinking. Image Three foregrounds the integral role of readiness to grapple with differences and complexities within the movement of individual and collective thinking. Finally, Image Four evidences readiness as rising to the needs of situations, empowering agency and responsibility gained through ownership of the ideas underway. It seems that the potential within teaching indirectly insists on Dewey's (1938) characterization of control or direction as emerging from within the learning experience itself and not from an external imposition. Hansen terms such control "kinetic," liberating learners and learning rather than confining them (Hansen, p. 43).

Collectively, these four images reveal educators' and students' liberation as they journey into a formative, curricular landscape with increasing control and direction found within process itself. Educators and their students navigate roomy paths of self-formation and discovery that embrace method-in-the-making—growing selves that inhabit postures of questioning, scrutinizing, analyzing, discerning, reflecting, speculating, adapting, changing, and building, all the while inspiring and guiding the discourse, and breathing vitality into learning. In other words, educators and students find much sustenance for individual and collective growth and well-being. But the primary responsibility for educators is to assume the cocurricular conditions and ongoing attention to the individual and collective movement of thinking in classrooms (Dewey, 1938; Hansen, 1995). An inquiry stance on the part of educators and their students, one that values curiosity, experimentation, adaptation, diversity, and even mistakes, thus creates potential pathways to learning. Thus, curricular method-in-the-making takes shape through the following responsive meaning-making modes:

- Building dialogical multivoiced conversations that foster enlarged and deepened thinking and transformation;
- Unmasking diversities; contributing to communities strengthened through attention to diversities, rather than fearing them;
- Practicing the creation of fluid, purposeful learning encounters across all disciplines and interests; negotiating difficult knowledge through seeking learner/learning connectedness and sustaining genuine inquiry;

- Recovering individual and collective trust, pleasure and pride, within the processes of learning.

Given that these responsive meaning-making modes are often neglected, concrete practice alongside professional supports and resources are essential for guiding, steering, and confidence-building among educators, students, and associated communities (Hansen, 2001a, 2005, 2011; Macintyre Latta, 2004, 2013; Rodgers, 2020; Sherman, 2013).

Again, and again, educational institutions and communities struggle to foster and support the responsive meaning-making modes these images of practice vivify. It is the act of continually locating and navigating meaning-making, eliciting sensibilities and responsibilities for inquiry, that ultimately shapes the learning contexts within the conduct of activities. To be clear, it is not the activities themselves that occasion meaning-making matters. Rather, the images of practice conveyed in this chapter offer a conception of teaching through curricular enactment that attend to the particulars of students, context, and subject matter, placing trust in process as well as in educators' and students' capacities within process. This is the nature of method that allows educators and students to begin to gain the confidence found within the specifics of curricular situations and interactions, suggesting worthwhile learning directions. Confidence in process demands that educators and students be able to articulate why, how, and what they are orienting their practices toward, and to embody these ways of being within their lived practices. What participating educators and students experience is just how revolutionary knowledge-making can be, holding learning powers and possibilities discovered by way of the associated sensibilities and responsibilities of curricular enactment when method is oriented toward growth, greater self-understanding, enhanced well-being, and the opportunity to continually situate self in the world alongside others. The images of practice depicted above help elucidate just what these sensibilities and responsibilities include the following:

Method-in-the-Making's Relationality

Educators, and in turn students, cultivate a sensibility toward more and more willingness to attend to social, historical, cultural, political, and personal experiences, perspectives, and contexts, which influence and interact within every situation. In doing so, the relational complexities human beings bring to all sense-making are foregrounded and embraced as elemental human resources holding the genesis for inquiry of all kinds. These relational complexities challenge us to formulate self-understandings, values, assumptions, and beliefs, thus helping to foster learning contexts in which to responsibly and respectfully grapple with relationships.

Method-in-the-Making's Generativity

Educators and students cultivate a sensibility toward entering and dwelling within the relationships present and already at play within situations. In doing so, seeing and acting within educative situations attends to the generative process that knowledge-making invites. Suggestions unfold, and are negotiated, as paths of inquiry open up. Such openings invest in the "powers and purposes of those taught" (Dewey, 1938, p. 45). Not to do so, as Dewey points out, would be "to neglect the place of intelligence in the development and control of a living and moving experience" (Dewey, p. 88). These powers and purposes may take multiple forms, but revering and conversing from these given powers and purposes, as the material for knowledge-making, forms the responsive and responsible ground of genuine inquiry.

Method-in-the-Making's Need of Other(s)

Educators and students cultivate a sensibility toward the significant ways in which other(s) call personal understandings into question, valuing interactions, debates, and deliberations, remaining always in need of other ideas, experiences, perspectives, and understandings. Personal needs and interests initially direct efforts. These efforts are then redirected as individuals convey and begin to attend to the relations they meet and negotiate, as thinking with and through others is made more accessible. Understandings are reached and extended. The evolving inquiry is not simply the workings of an individual's interiority, but rather is responsibly inclusive of the narratives and reflections of others.

Method-in-the-Making's Temporal/Spatial Agency

Educators and students cultivate a sensibility toward temporality, to the past-present-future interplay within every situation, positioning all involved to respond to the relational and interactive connections that ensue through following the unfolding inquiry. Dewey (1934) characterizes such unfolding connections as derived "about, within, and without and through repeated visits" (Dewey, p. 229). And it is these gathering connections that hold the contingencies that educators, students, and communities must understand as the risks and opportunities worthy of curricular negotiation. Dewey (1938) explains that it is the sustenance gained through such understanding that occasions the kind of present that "has a favourable effect upon the future" (Dewey, p. 50). Curricular connections attending to the potential in the present, invest in individual and collective growth that responsibly sees and acts within the temporality at play and within the given circumstances.

Method-in-the-Making's Interdependency with Imagination

Educators and students cultivate a sensibility toward imagination as a gateway to knowledge-making, acting as a way to envision the potential in situations, in self, and in other(s), rather than as a distinct specialized faculty of the mind. Dewey (1934) claims that such participatory knowledge-making through thinking, feeling, seeing, and acting "illuminates" (Dewey, p. 22) understandings and fosters internalized responsibility, instilling embodied comprehension, fundamental to being human.

The interrelated sensibilities and associated responsibilities of relationality, generativity, need of other(s), temporal/spatial agency, and imagination invite the individual and collective meaning-making that Hansen (2001a) characterizes as teaching indirectly. The ongoing reciprocal nature of teaching indirectly conveyed within the images of practice actively assume individual and collective openness alongside a commitment to attend to ensuing interactions. Thus, it is through individual and collective traversing of the knowledge-making terrain that deliberation, intuition, anticipation, new ideas, and enlarged understandings prompt interactions and compel participants' investment and ongoing attention. And it is only by traversing the exposed methodological terrain, providing access to, and practice with, these sensibilities and responsibilities that the participating educators and I envision the kinds of knowledge-making happening in education and communities that will foster meaning-making that matters. It is such matters, embodying and strengthening the roles of education within all institutions, communities, and beyond, that participating educators and students portrayed in the images of practice described in this chapter concretely encountered, reorienting method as necessarily responsive, and invigorating learning for all.

ACKNOWLEDGMENTS

This chapter draws on research supported by the Social Sciences and Humanities Research Council of Canada. Cette recherche a été subventionnée par le Conseil de recherches en sciences humaines au Canada.

The authors would also like to acknowledge the deep care and commitment of participating school district, educators, and students undertaking this research project.

NOTE

1. The specific public school setting and the provincial curriculum mandate support the development of inquiry-oriented learning experiences. Educators are encouraged to reformulate their practices oriented toward deeper learning, flexibility to build on particular strengths and needs, concern for the big ideas undergirding and integrating all subject matter, with assessment as an ongoing accompaniment of learning. See https://curriculum.gov.bc.ca/.

REFERENCES

Dewey, J. (1910a). Science as subject-matter and as method. *Science, 31*(787), 121–127.

Dewey, J. (1910b). *How we think*. D.C. Heath & Co. Publishers.

Dewey, J. (1916). *Democracy and education*. Macmillan Company.

Dewey, J. (1934). *Art as experience*. Capricorn Books.

Dewey, J. (1938). *Experience and education*. Touchstone.

Hansen, D. T. (1995). *The call to teach*. Teachers College Press.

Hansen, D. T. (2001). *Exploring the moral heart of teaching: Toward a teacher's creed*. Teachers College Press.

Hansen, D. T. (2005). Creativity in teaching and building a meaningful life as a teacher. *Journal of Aesthetic Education, 39*(2), 57–68.

Hansen, D. T. (2011). *The teacher and the world: A study of cosmopolitanism as education*. Routledge.

Macintyre Latta, M. (2004). Retrieving possibilities: Confronting a forgetfulness and deformation of teaching/learning methodology. *Teachers and Teaching: Theory and Practice, 10*(3), 329–344.

Macintyre Latta, M. (2013). *Curricular conversations: Play is the (missing) thing*. Routledge.

Macintyre Latta, M. (2018, April 27). Field notes.

Rodgers, C. R. (2020). *The art of reflective teaching*. Teachers College Press.

Sherman, S. (2013). *Teacher preparation as an inspirational practice: Building capacities for responsiveness*. Routledge.

CHAPTER 4

The Art of Living, or the Aesthetic Dimension of Teaching

Hansjörg Hohr

Ideas about what it means to be human constitute the basis of education. Such ideas are moral in that they reflect our hopes for the kinds of persons we wish for children to become. David Hansen discusses the moral in education through the twin perspectives of "an image of the growing person" (2001, p. 41) and "the art of living as an educational outlook" (2011, p. 32). While these perspectives have much in common, the first concentrates on our hopes for children, while the second focuses on who we want educators to be. In this chapter I focus on Hansen's ideas on the aesthetic dimensions of teaching. What we wish for our children inevitably bears on the question of who teachers should be. In teaching the "art of living" to students, teachers themselves are also called to master this art.

GROWTH AND COMMUNICATION

In *The Call to Teach* (1995), Hansen reconstructs the idea of teaching as a vocation or calling. Teaching thus differs from occupations and professions narrowly construed in terms of producing, selling, and earning. The decisive feature of teaching as vocation is the constitutive role of personhood in teaching. Personhood features in two ways: first, there is the "sense of self, of personal identity" and "personal fulfillment" (Hansen, 1995, p. 3) that derive from teaching. Though typically performed within institutions, teaching often transcends the formal frames. The teachers Hansen describes in *The Call to Teach* are dedicated to their craft—they engage with colleagues, read scholarship in pedagogy and education, and develop courses and curriculum. They endure various hardships—administrative chores, emotionally taxing confrontations, disappointments, mistakes, doubts, and constraining workplace conditions. In short, being a teacher proves to be more of a way of life than a mere job. These teachers, as Hansen puts it, *inhabit* their lives as teachers (Hansen, 1995, p. 13).

Personhood helps us frame teaching as involving the whole person. The teachers in Hansen's study have their own style, their unique concerns and challenges. To observe one teacher from the next is, for Hansen, as if one were entering a completely different world (1995, p. 115). The personal imprint teachers make on classroom proceedings is considerable. Certainly, teachers exercise a broad repertoire of techniques, though teaching cannot be reduced to the merely technical. The subject of teaching is the communication between the participants—not of a single individual but in the exchange between persons. Nor is teaching reducible to the implementation of policies, rules, or the execution of assignments and tasks. Rather, teaching is about "shaping an environment" (Hansen, 2001, p. 80), which at its core is an aesthetic activity.

Hansen's subsequent book, *The Moral Heart of Teaching* (2001), alludes to the aesthetic through the play on the term *heart*, which contains the term *art*. The title suggests that the moral is the life force of teaching, also implying its status as an art. Moreover, heart connotes sensuousness and emotion, which are often viewed in opposition to the moral, whereas Hansen is suggesting emotion as intrinsic to the moral. This connection is expressed through Hansen's notion of moral sensibility. The ideas of *moral sensibility* and *shaping the learning environment* throughout the text resonate through allusions to the sphere of art and aesthetics. In several instances, Hansen connects teaching to poetry and architecture, frequently using the term *artful* to describe the nature of the teacher's work.

AESTHETIC QUALITY OF EXPERIENCE

A promising approach to understanding the aesthetic is offered by John Dewey, a wellspring of inspiration for Hansen. Dewey's significance resides in how he negotiates the aesthetic within a vast framework of human experience, thus highlighting the continuity between the aesthetic and everyday life. Here I share with Dewey this methodological point of departure, namely that experience is decisive in defining the relationship between the human being and the world. Since teaching is part of everyday life, Dewey's conception of the aesthetic may help us deepen our understanding of teaching.

Dewey develops the idea of the aesthetic in the context of the relationship between an organism and its environment. Life is viewed as a *continuous* and *rhythmic* alternation of phases of disruption and participation, of strife and harmony. One phase of life is not to be had without the other. Dewey writes, "And when the participation comes after a phase of disruption and conflict, it bears within itself the germs of a consummation akin to the esthetic" (Dewey, 1934, p. 15). Much like our scientific endeavors, the aesthetic can also be understood as a negotiation between organism and environment. Typically, the artist and scientist differ in emphasis, the artist caring more for union while the scientist places emphasis on resolving the problematic, where "tension between the matter of observation and of thought is marked" (Dewey, p. 15). This difference, however, is only a matter of degree, as the scientist likewise aims at resolution while the artist is similarly spurred by dissonance and conflict.

The nature of the aesthetic can also be grasped in the terms of intellectual experience. Likening intellectual experience to a stormy ocean, Dewey writes:

> [There] are a series of waves; suggestions reaching out and being broken in a clash, or being carried onwards by a cooperative wave. If a conclusion is reached, it is that of a movement of anticipation and cumulation, one that finally comes to completion. Hence an experience of thinking has its own esthetic quality. (Dewey, 1934, p. 38)

The aesthetic shares with the intellectual qualities of anticipation, cumulation, and consummation of experience. The only significant difference between the intellectual and the aesthetic is that the materials of the latter consist of qualities, while the materials of the former "are signs or symbols having no intrinsic quality of their own" (Dewey, 1934, p. 38). The intellectual experience has "a satisfying emotional quality because it possesses internal integration and fulfillment reached through ordered and organized movement. This artistic structure may be immediately felt. In so far, it is esthetic" (Dewey, p. 38). In the stormy ocean example above, "the movement of anticipation and cumulation . . . that finally comes to completion" is complemented or, perhaps, contradicted, by the "ordered and organized movement" that renders "internal integration and fulfillment" and "a satisfying emotional quality" to the experience. Dewey comprises these qualities in the term *artistic structure* (Dewey, p. 38).

The aesthetic here is tied to the fact that this structure is "immediately felt" as "the internal integration and fulfillment." The "insofar" that follows might raise doubt as to Dewey's meaning. Are there artistic structures that are not immediately felt and therefore not aesthetic? Are there other structures of experience that are immediately felt and thus aesthetic? Perhaps the term *esthetic phase* of experience that Dewey uses several times may cast light on the issue: "The esthetic or undergoing phase of experience is receptive. It involves surrender" (Dewey, 1934, p. 53). In this instance, the aesthetic is synonymous with the modification and development of mental structures. Harmony is reestablished when the mental structures are brought in alignment with the environment.

Taking Dewey's *Art as Experience* as a whole, it is important to consider the aesthetic quality as a measure of internal integration, differentiation, and complexity of experience. These structural qualifications comprise "unity," the "satisfying emotional quality" that accompanies "rhythm" (Dewey, 1934, pp. 134–186), "flow" (Dewey, p. 36), and, eventually, "fulfillment" in the resolution of the conflict or the problem.

SHAPING THE ENVIRONMENT

For Dewey, there is no experience unless there is expression. Experience unfolds along a process of expression. While "experience" refers to mental processes and structures, "expression" refers to the respective interaction between organism and environment. The result of expression is the expressive object—whether performance or artifact—which means that the expressive object is experienced by others in the act of perception.

Dewey proceeds to distinguish statements from expressions. A statement carries meaning by pointing to situations where an experience may be had. "But there are other meanings that present themselves directly as possessions of objects which are experienced. There is no need for a code or convention of interpretation; the meaning is as inherent in immediate experience as is that of a flower garden" (Dewey, 1934, p. 83). The meaning of the expressive object is not ready-made and cannot be taken without further ado. It has to be reconstructed in perception. The decisive point is that experience in everyday life is constantly threatened by "distraction and dispersion" (Dewey, p. 35), while the expressive object offers the opportunity for an enhanced experience where all that is random, irrelevant, and distracting is removed. With the concept of the expressive object, Dewey conceptualizes what the teaching and learning situation is about. It is about construction of the expressive object as a "conjoint" activity between teacher and students, the construction of a structured environment, and of improved situations with respect to form and content, thus offering learning opportunities that everyday life seldom does.

Hansen's notion of "indirect teaching" touches on Dewey's idea of the expressive object. It is a notion inspired by both Rousseau (1979) and Dewey (1916). In his *Émile*, Rousseau distinguishes among three "masters" in education: nature, persons, and things. By observing that inanimate things impart meaning, Rousseau essentially invents the modern concept of education by showing that teaching first and foremost consists of arranging situations where children may have educative experiences. Thus, the master in *Émile* minimizes his direct interventions and recasts the role as director of learning situations. "You will not be master of the child if you are not the master of all that surrounds him" (Rousseau, 1979, p. 95). Rousseau goes to extreme lengths to arrange situations where Émile has educational experiences. Even more astonishing is the control regime within which Rousseau's theory of education is formulated:

> Emile is an orphan. It makes no difference whether he has his father or mother. Charged with their duties, I inherit all their rights. He must honor his parents, but he ought to obey only me. That is my first or, rather, my sole condition. (Rousseau, 1979, pp. 52–53)

Hansen may be correct in describing the master of Rousseau's text as a "heroic miracle worker" (Hansen, 2001, p. 70). While minimizing direct control, the educator totalizes control over the environment where almost every aspect is artificial, though appearing natural to the child. Throughout *Emile*, Rousseau underlines the difference between learning from experience and direct instruction. He argues forcefully that teaching didactically will either have no effect or, worse still, will destroy the child's natural curiosity, initiative, and sense of agency, altogether exercising children in meaninglessness and inducing in them a dislike toward learning, thus inspiring animus toward the adult. The critical problem with this kind of education, however, is that in making it appear as though every outcome of the teacher's action were a natural consequence, one removes the chance for legitimate objections to be made by the student. After all, you cannot argue with nature.

A century following Rousseau, Dewey serves as the most prominent and momentous promoter of experience in education. With Dewey, the emphasis moves to the social and symbolic dimensions of experience. Whereas Rousseau tries to isolate his pupil from society, and delay contact with texts until adolescence, for Dewey experience is initiated by the student through social and symbolic mediation. In this way, Dewey places communication at the center of education. Hansen notes the difference between Rousseau and Dewey on this score when he writes: "Dewey's perspective helps turn the teacher's gaze away from him- or herself and toward the classroom environment and the diverse factors that figure into its emergence" (Hansen, 2001, p. 70).

It is not that Dewey's perspective on the learning environment is less demanding or less comprehensive than Rousseau's. Rather, Dewey's perspective on the environment takes a dramatic shift. From now on the environment is viewed not only in a material sense, but in a social one. The main criterion for successful education now becomes successful communication. Rousseau's disdain for the written word in early education is no longer viable from Dewey's perspective. Rousseau's controlling educator must yield to the obvious learning opportunities that the child's social context affords, and at last consider the wealth of symbolic materials available.

Dewey's reflections on the act and object of expression converge with Hansen's reflections on the art of living. Much like the German neo-humanistic tradition of *Bildung*, Hansen also emphasizes self-improvement as a central feature of the art of living. The emphasis is balanced by an equal emphasis on environmental factors and social responsibility. For teachers initiating students to the art of living, the environment is a central concern. Hansen thus compares teachers to architects, shaping the learning environment to meet the needs, wants, and expectations of its inhabitants (Hansen, 1995, p. 116). This comparison offers significant points to consider. For one, teachers make important contributions to creating a learning space for their students. Such space is under consistent pressure from two sides, from the past and the future. There is a tradition to pass on, and there is also an "end-in-view" with respect to whom students are becoming. In between these formidable powers the present moment comes under threat, needing protection. The metaphor of the teacher as architect gives expression to the teacher's attention to the here and now.

In considering the activities of the classroom as objects of expression, shaped by both teacher and students, one takes note of the aesthetic dimension of curriculum as well. This aesthetic dimension is often recognized in the teaching of language, poetry, and literature, as well as the fine and performing arts. Subjects such as science and mathematics, however, do not traditionally acknowledge their inherent aesthetic features, even though playfulness and sensuousness, for example, often accompany the study of both subjects. School should therefore assist children with the multitude of aesthetic choices in everyday life, starting with the question of relating to their own bodies as both medium of communication and biological organism.

The shift away from direct to indirect teaching actualizes two restraints. The first is an impediment, the other a precondition. The first concerns the systemic limitations of most schools. When they are measured by Dewey's concept of experience, one cannot help realize that most schools decontextualize the learning process, entailing a desertlike impoverishment of experience. This peculiarity of the institution of the school was noticed at its outset in Europe by Jan Amos Comenius (1592–1670). While in school we look, talk, read, and write about the world, we do not experience it through direct interaction. The progressivist movement in the United States, and the reform movement in Europe, tried to counteract this systemic problem, achieving modest success. The question becomes, then, how teachers today might meet these systemic limitations.

The second restraint regards the delineation of the teachers' role. The emphasis on indirect teaching would, on first glance, appear as exonerating teachers. Hansen points out that instead of attempting everything by themselves, teachers can rely instead on complex situations and activities in order to promote learning (Hansen, 2001, p. 70). On a second look, however, a daunting expansion of challenges comes into view as the whole environment of the young must now be considered by the teacher as a potential domain of educational activity.

MORAL SENSIBILITY

Hansen's idea of moral sensibility supplements his idea of indirect teaching and refers to "conduct" as the basis of teaching. Conduct, in Hansen's view, expresses and reveals the character of a person (Hansen, 2001, p. 29). It is the person's unique way of being in and orientation toward the world.

Hansen ties conduct to a person's sense of agency, relating conduct to personalized patterns of behavior. Moral sensibility can be understood to be such a pattern.

As an initial approach, Hansen proposes the term *moral sensibility* as a way "to bring reason and emotion together" (Hansen, 2001, p. 32). A more elaborate explanation the author offers through the terms *sympathetic sensibility* and *thoughtful emotion*. The first relates to "reasoning and foresight in which the welfare of other people, not just of oneself, is front and center" (Hansen, p. 32). Even though the etymology of the term *sympathetic sensibility* points in the direction of emotions—to feel with others, and perceptivity of the emotions of others—Hansen instead focuses on the cognitive aspect of caring for others. Reason and emotion are thus brought together when reasoning is led and moved by regard for the welfare of others. This includes the teachers' ability and willingness to perceive their own emotions as well as that of their students. Moreover, it requires emotional strength and a willingness to endure the taxing emotions that are often part and parcel of the work.

Such emotional strength is a precondition for the second term Hansen considers, *thoughtful emotion*, which refers to teachers' reflection on how to act so as to further student welfare. It calls for a certain emotional distance in order to not be overcome by situations. Instead, one is to keep a clear head and reflect on what course of action the situation calls for. Here the emphasis is placed on action that furthers the welfare of others, not an aloofness, or standing apart, but "to stand back from a classroom situation" (Hansen, 2001, p. 33).

In order to illustrate the concept of moral sensibility, Hansen asks us to imagine two different kinds of teachers offering identical lessons: one does so in an offhand way, without much expectation from students or interest in subject matter; while the other teacher presents enthusiastically, thus "expressing her involvement in teaching and her confidence in her students' power to learn" (Hansen, 2001, p. 33). The latter teacher is thus a model of moral sensitivity for displaying a keen interest in both her students and the lesson. In short, the latter teacher combines reason with emotion.

Bringing reason and emotion together leads Hansen to consider the concept of *moral grace*. Under this heading Hansen describes a musician's recollection of the moral impact that her fervently engaged teacher made. Here the music teacher, Nadia Boulanger, is able to convey to her student, Suzanne Hoover, the deeply felt joy that concentration, hard work, patience, and deliberation may lead to.

Moral grace also serves as an important concept in the philosophy of Friedrich Schiller, where it evokes a synthesis of reason and emotion. With Schiller, moral grace concerns the way in which individuals constitute themselves, with special consideration, both theoretically and practically, for how the physical and spiritual nature of human beings might come together.

Schiller looks to the realm of aesthetics and to play where the self discovers its freedom and constitutes itself. In the aesthetic realm, neither instinct nor reason has anything at stake, and thus has nothing to defend. Though emotion and reason are active in the aesthetic realm, they are free to let go of the reins and start to befriend each other. This process of reconciliation between reason and emotion culminates in the "beautiful soul," which, according to Schiller (2005), is defined by moral grace. Whereas in the realm of action instinct and reason permanently fight for supremacy, the person who has reached a state of moral grace carries out their duties as if induced by instinct. Thus, it is not the single action of the person that is moral, but the whole character (Schiller, p. 152). As such, moral grace becomes the supreme educational goal for Schiller (1967). It implies a lifetime of work expanding the aesthetic realm at the expense of the realm of action as dictated by moral law. The example of the enthusiastic and encouraging teacher discussed above has moral grace in that she is not only fulfilling a duty but following an inclination, or, rather in such a teacher duty has transformed into inclination. The doings of the beautiful soul, by contrast, are guided by the person herself. Freedom is made possible by the correspondence of instinct and moral law, though Schiller is realistic enough to concede that even in the instance of a highly developed moral grace, there may arise unresolvable contradictions, in which case reason must take command.

Hansen presents several examples of teachers addressing emotionally taxing events in the classroom, like the suicide of a classmate, or the shooting of a student. Such examples are presented under the heading of *moral presence* (2001, pp. 35–38). These teachers invite students to talk through unsettling and confusing experiences. We can say that this invitation flows from the moral grace of teachers who aspire to unite reason and emotion in both themselves and their students. By talking through upsetting and traumatic events, students are given the chance to clarify their emotions and recuperate their subjectivity through self-reflection, an opportunity that might otherwise become suffocated under the onslaught of emotions. Hansen refers to such practices, and with good reason, as moral presence since these teachers aim at furthering their students' ability to act. Here Hansen echoes Schiller's conception of moral grace as an education of the emotions through communication and reflection so that our emotions become something we enact and achieve, and not that which happens to us.

Teachers who embody moral presence will regard the education of the emotions as a central educational task, and as the basis of the independence of their students. Naturally, emotions have the potential to disturb or disrupt the work with subject matter, but they are also present at some level in everything students do. They should be regarded not only as potentially valuable, but as indispensable resources in the classroom, even though their cultivation presents to teachers perhaps the most difficult and challenging task of all.

The education of the emotions is difficult to keep in view, especially in light of the institutional demands on teachers, and the often formidable demands of the subject matter itself. Under the pressures of institutional requirements with respect to students' academic achievement, and in the fervor and enthusiasm for a certain subject matter, the students' emotions and their outlook on the world can easily be lost.

Several other topics in Hansen's reflections on teaching resonate with Schiller's aesthetic. One of these is Hansen's remarks on naivete, which in Schiller's view is a hallmark of moral grace (Schiller, 1983, p. 24). Schiller distinguishes between two kinds of naivete. One form of naivete is due to the dominance of emotion and to a lack of experience. The other kind of naivete, however, is based on thorough knowledge of the world and its moral shortcomings, which nevertheless preserves a moral simplicity and straightforwardness. Such a disposition features in our vision of the growing person and can be considered a central ideal in teaching as well. Certainly, teachers could do without naivete if every student entered school full of trust and gratitude, of enthusiasm and curiosity, of eagerness to learn and a limitless appetite for understanding the world. As we know, the reality is that many students come to school predisposed to distrust adults, and with more faith in the possibilities of power and material gain than in knowledge and reflection. Or they succumb to the pathologies of the institution itself, caring more for grades than for knowledge, feigning interest and compliance, aiming more to please the teacher instead of cultivating their interests, eventually resigning themselves to meaninglessness (Fenstermacher, 2006). The naive teacher is aware of all these problems and still maintains a moral stance, working tirelessly and unperturbed toward winning the trust of students, on kindling their interest in knowledge, on opening new worlds to them, and on sharing the joys that these worlds offer.

EDUCATION AND ART, CONCLUDING REMARKS

In the concluding chapter of *The Call to Teach* (1995, pp. 137–161), Hansen considers arguments in opposition to using vocation to describe teaching, mainly on the grounds of the existing societal conditions in which teachers work. These critics point to overpowering social forces that suppress the evolvement of human subjectivity, and where balance between individual and societal concern is lost. Such arguments are reminiscent of the Frankfurt School, from Theodor Adorno's observation of the *non-identical*—or how uniqueness is increasingly discouraged by society (Adorno, 2005, pp. 192–193) to Jürgen Habermas's (1984) observation of the invasion of the life world by the system world. With respect to the systemic conditions of teaching, one can point to the increasing external regulation of schools, the introduction of internationally standardized tests, and other parameters that curtail the freedom of teachers.

In spite of these systemic problems, Hansen suggests that we would do well to keep in mind the opportunities the educational system still provides. I sympathize with this pragmatic stance and would add that emphasizing the central role of personhood in teaching is an essential argument to make to policymakers inclined to leave ample space to the discretion of teachers.[1] Since personhood is a central concern with respect to both teachers and students, I think that the aesthetic quality of teaching is indispensable to the concept of teaching. Neither in the realm of reason nor of emotions alone is there adequate space for the development of personal autonomy. It is the space where reason and emotion are brought together, however, where the person constitutes themselves.

For a long time, I was opposed to the idea of conceiving teaching as an art. One impediment was the thought that while artists shape aesthetic objects, teachers shape students. Such a thought seemed to be a category mistake—students are persons and aims in themselves, they are not objects of manipulation. When I realized that teachers are not manipulating students but shaping learning situations, it became possible to envision learning situations as objects of art. Still, I share Hansen's caution with respect to declaring teaching as an art in the modern sense of the word (2001, p. 135). There is a decisively valid difference between art and teaching in that the former is measured by its contribution to cultural growth, while the latter is measured with respect to its contribution to individual growth.

Furthermore, these differences in aims have consequences for the relationship to subject matter. The artist works on the borders of the culturally known in order to expand those borders and to open paths into formerly unknown territory. The artist studies their object relentlessly, with an unblinking eye, until the object surrenders its secrets. In doing so they cannot and must not worry whether the public will understand their work, and indeed the history of art is full of examples of how new aesthetic discoveries are first met with incomprehension, even antagonism. Nonetheless, in the long run, the validity criterion of art is whether it makes life more understandable and more meaningful to the public.

Quite different is the relationship of teaching to its subject matter. The purpose of teaching is the growth of individuals. Put differently, teaching is the arrangement of a meeting between individual students and human culture, with the aim of the critical appropriation of culture by students. Thus, teachers approach culture not with the aim of expanding it, but with what the continental tradition of philosophy would call its didactic purpose, asking, "What is the meaning of a given cultural content for the present life of students? What is the meaning of the same for their future, and how might I, as a teacher, make it meaningful for students?" (Klafki, 2000).

Teaching may not be art, but it is certainly an aesthetic activity in the senses of both Dewey and Schiller. In the Deweyan sense, teaching works at shaping a learning activity, along with its preconditions, in such a way so as to minimize the threats of dispersion and distraction and to further its "flow," "rhythm," and "unity." Teaching in this sense is enhancing the aesthetic quality of experience. Teaching is an aesthetic activity in Schiller's sense in that it aims at bringing knowledge and morality, reason and emotion together, furthering the autonomy and subjectivity of the student.

NOTE

1. Hansen devotes a whole book to the idea of teaching as a call, or vocation. I have no alternative to offer, but am still not convinced by this choice. Already the juxtaposition of the terms shows the power of established meanings. While *vocation* is pointing toward the training for crafts, the term *call* has strong ecclesiastic and religious connotations, and one wonders whether it is enough to declare that this connotation is unintentional. Also, the question of who is calling appears not to find a satisfactory answer. Hansen proposes that the call might issue from the practice of teaching itself. But then all occupations would be able to claim to be a call since they all are based on practices. Finally, not to follow a call would mean to fail oneself in a fundamental way. Could it be otherwise?

REFERENCES

Adorno, T. (2005). Education after Auschwitz. In T. Adorno (Ed.), *Critical models: Interventions and catchwords* (pp. 191–204). (H. W. Pickford, Trans.). Columbia University Press.

Dewey, J. (1916). *Democracy and education*. Macmillan Company.

Dewey, J. (1934). *Art as experience*. Capricorn Books.

Fenstermacher, G. (2006). Rediscovering the student in *Democracy and Education*. In D. T. Hansen (Ed.), *John Dewey and our educational prospect: A critical engagement with Dewey's Democracy and education* (pp. 97–112). State University of New York Press.

Hansen, D. T. (1995). *The call to teach*. Teachers College Press.

Hansen, D. T. (2001). *Exploring the moral heart of teaching: Toward a teacher's creed*. Teachers College Press.

Hansen, D. T. (2011). *The teacher and the world: A study of cosmopolitanism as education*. Routledge.

Klafki, W. (2000). The significance of classical theories of bildung for a contemporary concept of allgemeinbildung. In I. Westbury, K. Riquarts, & S. Hopmann (Eds.), *Teaching as a reflective practice: The German didaktik tradition* (pp. 85–107). L. Erlbaum Associates.

Rousseau, J.-J. (1979). *Émile, or On education* (A. Bloom, Trans.). Basic Books. (Original work published 1762)

Schiller, F. W. (1967). *On the aesthetic education of man in a series of letters* (E. M. Wilkinson & L. A. Willoughby, Trans.). Clarendon Press.

Schiller, F. W. (1983). *On the naïve and sentimental in literature* (H. Watanabe-O'Kelly, Trans.). Carcanet New Press.

Schiller, F. W. (2005). On grace and dignity (J. V. Curran, Trans.). In J. V. Curran & C. Fricker (Eds.), *Schiller's "On grace and dignity" in its cultural context: Essays and a new translation* (pp. 123–170). Camden House.

CHAPTER 5

Education as the Art of Living

David Hansen's Work and Its Relevance to China's Education Reform

Huajun Zhang

All birds have flown away, so high,
A lonely cloud drifts on, so free.
Mutual gaze both not tired, the Mount and I,
Nor I of him, nor he of me.[1]

—Li Bai (701-762)

INTRODUCTION

I first encountered David Hansen's work when I served as his Chinese translator for a keynote speech he delivered at Beijing Normal University, where I am currently a faculty member. The year was 2014, and Hansen had just completed the fieldwork for his project "The Person in the World." In his address, Hansen proposed a familiar question in a compelling way: Who is a "good" teacher? I still remember how the main point of the speech struck me, as well as many in the audience: The "role" does not teach, but the person does. He delivered the speech with a humane tone and sensibility. As a young scholar, I felt encouraged and spiritually uplifted in knowing that there could be scholarship like this. More importantly, I felt that I shared with Hansen a deep concern for the human condition in a rapidly changing and conflicted world.[2] In a time when most educational research is measured by quantifiable standards, we seemed to stand together for the possibility of human flourishing, focusing instead on the day-to-day practice of teaching and learning in educational settings.

Now, writing this chapter on Hansen offers me the chance to return to his work in a more systematic way. Reading through Hansen's research, from the early stages of his scholarly life in the late 1980s to the present day, is like having a dialogue with my own obscure passion for educational stud- ies. While painstakingly seeking a way, and determined to be alone to some extent, I deeply appreciate Hansen's company, both through his work and through his embodied practice as a patient, receptive, and passionate teach- er. Through the wonder and concern for teaching, as evident in Hansen's academic writing from the very beginnings of his career, I also sense a con- sistent and persistent love of teaching, and of being in the world. His work evinces a desire to renew and enrich his own life through teaching, and through the study of teaching. In his works one can sense a faith that the vigor of life can be aroused and refreshed in the daily experience of teaching and learning. There is always something that shines even in the seemingly mundane aspects of life. I cherish this faith in the depths of my heart.

In what follows, I offer an interpretation of Hansen's work throughout his academic career. Particularly, I highlight his creative use of Dewey's idea of the immediate quality of experience and relate it to his recent work on "bearing witness" in teaching. Then I briefly discuss Hansen's ethics of self- cultivation and its connection to self-cultivation in the Chinese intellectual tradition. Finally, I relate Hansen's work to the challenges of contemporary Chinese education.

EDUCATION AS THE ART OF LIVING: TO BECOME A PERSON, NOT A ROLE

From his earliest publication on Socrates as a teacher (Hansen, 1988) to his current work on bearing witness (Hansen, 2018), Hansen offers a consistent but evolving perspective on education. Briefly put, education is about the art of living—a philosophy of action for becoming a better person in the world. To serve this ethical aim, teaching is understood as a deliberate and moral practice in which the teacher takes the lead to fashion environments in which students learn the art of living and to become better persons in the world.

Particularly during the 2000s when he moved to Teachers College, Columbia University, Hansen developed the idea of cosmopolitanism as an educative sensibility for dwelling in a radically changing and conflict- ing world (Hansen, 2011). If the idea of education as the art of living has everlasting value beyond the contemporary, his writing on cosmopolitanism in education reminds us to pay closer attention to the particular time in which we live. Hansen recognizes how the force of globalization permeates the daily lives of ordinary people, in which people are more susceptible to change, conflict, and a cultural homelessness due to either cultural relativ- ism or extreme conservatism. In a world where the comfort of holding to a secure set of values can no longer be taken for granted, the urgent task of education becomes helping the young build a sense of home by creating a new space in which they can maintain loyalty to local tradition while remaining open to the new possibilities that an increasingly interconnected world offers (Hansen, 2010a).

THE PERSON, NOT THE ROLE, WHO TEACHES

As early as 1988, with the article "Was Socrates a Socratic Teacher?," Hansen addresses the apparent teacher-student relationship between Socrates and Theaetetus. From the evolving dialogue between the two, Hansen observes that "the apparent roles of teacher and student have almost merged into one: the roles, if they ever existed, have almost disappeared" (Hansen, 1988, p. 222). In a 1992 article, "The Emergence of a Shared Morality in a Classroom," Hansen claims even more explicitly: "I will also suggest that the symbolic and moral meaning of classroom practice depends centrally on how we regard the person who occupies the role of teacher" (Hansen, 1992, p. 346). Then the focus becomes sharper in the 1993 article "From Role to Person: The Moral Layeredness of Classroom Teaching" (Hansen, 1993). In fact, the notion of the personhood of the teacher remains a central concern in Hansen's work on the moral dimensions of teaching and teachers. In the 1998 article "The Importance of the Person in the Role of the Teacher," Hansen again brings the theme to the forefront (Hansen, 1998). In this 10-year period, we can see just how Hansen took great strides to make a simple but powerful argument: It is the teacher as person, not the role, who teaches. The central figure in the practice of teaching is the person who occupies the role.

Through close descriptions of classroom life, witnessed during numerous visits to schools, Hansen reveals the extent to which the qualities and values that adhere to the person constitute the teacher who teaches. This means, for example, that it is a quality and dimension of the person that allows the teacher to make essential, personal connections with students. Hansen offers a qualitative approach to thinking about teaching, breaking away from the conventional understanding of teaching as a profession with predetermined and codified skills and aptitudes. Indeed, teaching is worthwhile and rewarding, but not merely because it is a self-sacrificing endeavor of public service; it is also because it serves as a call from the teacher themselves, an outgrowth of the desire to build enduring and ethical relationships with young people. Teaching addresses the ethical needs of the teacher as much as it does those of the student (Hansen, 1995).

Hansen does not limit his arguments to the theoretical. Unlike the conventional philosophically oriented scholar, Hansen works comfortably in the field, in real-life classrooms and schools. His work attests to the real life of teachers and their students, and how they both creatively practice an embodied cosmopolitanism. From 2012 to 2014, Hansen, along with two of his doctoral students, conducted the project "The Person in the World." In this project, he took as a guiding question "What does it mean to be a person in the world today?" In particular, he asked, "What does it mean to be a person in the role of teacher (including the teacher educator)?" This study is a fusion of philosophical and field-based anthropology, conducted with 16 teachers in eight New York City schools. More details on this study, especially Hansen's employment of the idea of "bearing witness" as an approach for the study of teaching and teachers, will be discussed later in this chapter.

CHERISH THE FULLNESS OF THE PRESENT TO MAKE INDIVIDUALITY FLOURISH

In an interview I once conducted with Hansen, he explained to me the reason he deliberately chose the word *person* in his project "The Person in the World," instead of using words like *self, identity,* or *human being.* By using the word *person*, we indicate that becoming a person requires upbringing and education. We are born to be human beings, but we become persons only through education. Therefore, the word *person* emphasizes becoming, possibility, and potentiality (Hansen & Zhang, 2017). The notion of person in Hansen's work is close to Dewey's idea of individuality. Dewey (1931) discusses the idea of individuality, mainly in the later work *Individualism Old and New.* Dewey refers to individuality as "a potentiality, a capacity of development" (Dewey, p. 156). Dewey's remarks on individuality below beautifully echo Hansen's ideas of person-making and cosmopolitanism as education:

> To gain an integrated individuality, each of us needs to cultivate his own garden. But there is no fence about this garden: it is no sharply marked-off enclosure. Our garden is the world, in the angle at which it touches our own manner of being. By accepting the corporate and industrial world in which we live, and by thus fulfilling the pre-condition for interaction with it, we, who are also parts of the moving present, create ourselves as we create an unknown future. (Dewey, p. 158)

Both Dewey and Hansen highlight the fulfillment of potentiality in the moving present. The flourishing of individuality, or the experience of learning to become a person, is not an ideal that transcends the concrete and real. Both Hansen and Dewey suggest the need to have confidence in the powerful potential embedded in every present moment of daily life. Hansen expresses this faith in the present through his interpretation of Montaigne's work:

> Montaigne (has) . . . confidence that whatever happens, he can *live* it rather than merely endure, ignore, hate, or reject it. He does not know God and he

does not know Humanity, in the sense of grasping hard and fast the lineaments of human nature, whatever they might be. But he knows life, as both a relisher, sufferer, and student of it, and he believes that "our being" exists in the here and now and that we must learn "to enjoy"' it as "we ought." . . . Montaigne privileges the present, not because it is fleeting, but because it is full. (Hansen, 2002, pp. 139–140)

This is philosophy as the art of living. It is about the "impelling desire" (Dewey, 1984, p. 57) to fully live in the world to tirelessly cultivate one's humanity. In Hansen's words, "To be well-formed, it seems, involves a reordering of life so that it embodies respect among the variety of human tendencies, qualities, and aspirations" (Hansen, 2002, p. 150).

The flourishing of individuality is potentially realized in every present moment. When the dull, ordinary, habitual moment is rediscovered by the inquiring person, a new self is realized. It is a moment of serious attentiveness combined with humility, respect, modest kindliness, and listening (Hansen, 2002, p. 141). It is a moment of creativity. Hansen writes:

The person loses, forgets, or gives her or his self over to the moment and concrete situation. However, *in* that very action, the person finds or realizes a new self, a self now marked or substantiated by a new increment, or new depth—however subtle or modest—of attentiveness and responsiveness to the world. The person is that much more poised to be creative (Hansen, 2005, p. 62).

This attentiveness and responsiveness to the world is a kind of detachment. In this moment, the individual becomes so engaged with the world that they forget themselves. Thus, a new space is created for the arrival of a new self in the moment. This new self is not distinct or disconnected from the self of old, however. It is embodied in the present moment that connects the past and the future. The present moment is aesthetic, moral, and complete in itself. Because of the need to cherish the fullness of the present moment, Hansen considers his observations of the classroom and witnessing the passing moments of classroom life as necessary and critical. It is a moral and aesthetic witness. It is a call from Hansen's impelling desire to be there. It is a path for his own journey of becoming a person in the world, as a teacher and as a teacher educator.

To write about the orientation of "bearing witness" in the classroom, Hansen reflects on the artist Cézanne's deep forays into art: "A minute in the world's life passes! To paint it in its reality! And forget everything for that. *To become that minute, be the sensitive plate*" (Hansen, 2017a, p. 26). This inclination reminds me of the poem by Li Bai quoted at the beginning of this chapter. In the mutual gaze between the poet and the Mount, the poet merges into the world as a whole. Therefore, the relationship between the person and the Mount is not instrumental—only for the enjoyment of the view—but qualitative. In Hansen's view, thinking becomes the pondering of the miracle of being here and communicating with one another (Hansen, 2004). In this sense, this world becomes *my* world in this moment of engaging, even though this moment can be fleeting and ephemeral. Bearing witness becomes a deliberate effort to achieve integrity between the individual and the world, much like Cézanne's efforts in painting or Li Bai's meditation on the Mount. To witness teaching is to consider teaching as person-making in the world, and witnessing is a practice of the art of living.

BEARING WITNESS AND THE IMMEDIATE QUALITY OF EXPERIENCE

To some extent, Hansen had already anticipated the approach of "bearing witness" in the study of teaching with teachers much earlier than the project "The Person in the World." In his autobiographical essay "On Wonder" (Hansen, 2014), he traces his philosophical wonder back to his childhood, when he was a 6-year-old boy feeling the warm and wet sand tumble through his balled fist. As a child he cherished this kind of feeling of the experienced life, and refers to Dewey's idea of "the immediate quality of experience." He agrees with Dewey that "the immediate quality of experience decisively influences a person's sensibility and orientation toward the world" (Hansen, p. 117). Here, Hansen acutely picks up a critical point made by Dewey, which Dewey consistently develops throughout his philosophical career but made most explicit in his later works *Experience and Nature* (1958) and *Art as Experience* (1934). To be alive means that the individual being is actively transacting with the life of things around them (Garrison, 2001). In other words, there are countless precognitive aesthetic, emotional, and tactile responses to the immediate environment. Hansen suggests that these responses can evoke a sense of enduring wonder at the world (Hansen, 2014).

In touching on "the immediate quality of experience," which is the primary and most significant experience of the individual, Hansen considers teaching as an ongoing work of art. Like any artwork, teaching is rich, complex, and creative. Moreover, it is full of aesthetic and moral communication between persons. Hansen reveals a sincere sympathy and appreciation for what he witnesses in the classroom. Likewise, he believes that educational researchers ought to observe classrooms and replace "arrogance with humility, pride with modesty, hate with kindliness, and fanatical idealism with listening" (Hansen, 2002, p. 141). With such an orientation, the approach of "bearing witness" in the study of teaching and teachers becomes a natural outcome (Hansen, 2017a; 2017b; 2018).

In considering teaching qualitatively, Hansen believes that "the truth of teaching is in the feeling of it" (Hansen, 2017a, p. 28). However, from this it does not follow that to study teaching is a purely subjective enterprise.

It is crucial that the researcher, who bears witness to teaching, is seriously concerned about teaching as a practice. There ought to be present in the researcher a strong sense of sympathy for teaching and teachers. Moreover, the researcher has faith that good teaching may creatively happen at any possible moment. They believe that "good teaching continues to happen, even in the context of the present difficult environment" (Hansen, 2004, p. 121). In this way, Hansen problematizes the conventional position of the researcher as an expert offering pedagogical solutions. The researcher need not provide advice, evaluation, or criticism of the teacher. Nor is the researcher a special advocate working on the teacher's behalf. Instead, the researcher occupies a simple being there "among the teachers." Hansen writes, "I can ready myself for truth, and put myself under the sway of such truth, by opening myself to ethical proximity with teachers. I can be among them. . . . It can also mean to be surrounded by, in the company of, in the midst of, a member of: to be with, rather than standing off to the side" (Hansen, 2017a, p. 28).

But if the researcher has no obligation to give advice to teachers, or to help teachers improve their teaching, what is the value of the approach of "bearing witness"? In Hansen's view, when one enters the classroom to bear witness, one hands over power. In this way, bearing witness is different from performing an inquiry. The distinction between the two orientations is crucial: Inquiry is mainly directed and initiated by the researcher. But bearing witness is more receptive to what happens. It is not the deliberate attempt to "collect data" in accordance with a predetermined structure or outcome. To illustrate this point, Hansen borrows the example put forth by Merleau-Ponty, who cites André Marchand's remarks made in reference to the artist Paul Klee. Marchand writes:

> In a forest, I have felt many times over that it was not I who looked at the forest. Some days I felt that the trees were looking at me, were speaking to me. . . . I was there, listening. . . . I think that the painter must be penetrated by the universe and not want to penetrate it. . . . I expect to be inwardly submerged, buried. Perhaps I paint to break out. (Hansen, 2017b, p. 15)

It is only when the researcher is fully engaged and appreciative of the value of the qualitative moments in teaching, with humility, respect, modest kindliness, and listening, that they can hear and witness the good of teaching. With such full appreciation, the researcher builds an ethical relationship with the teacher as well. Bearing witness, the researcher observes a qualitative world, breaking through predefined ways of understanding teaching and learning. In Hansen's words, "Through heeding the quiet testimony of the everyday, the person acknowledges reality in a new key. The person transforms even as her or his horizon of reality broadens and deepens" (Hansen, 2017a, p. 11).

HANSEN'S ETHICAL APPROACH TO EDUCATION
ECHOES THE CHINESE TRADITION OF POETICS
IN THE PRACTICE OF SELF-CULTIVATION

Hansen's ethical approach to education, especially his recent notion of "bearing witness" to teaching and teachers, is quite radical when placed in a Chinese context. Some critics may consider his idea as overly romantic, absent of any instrumental value. They might claim that if the researcher is not deemed an expert, can there truly be value in educational research? I suggest, however, that Hansen's approach to educational research is indeed highly practical, and that his ideas actually possess a powerful potential for understanding those embedded values in the concrete situations of education in daily life. In this sense, education is a creative activity of teaching and learning that helps cultivate individuality. In one of his more significant articles, "A Poetics of Teaching," Hansen describes "poetics" as this rich potentiality of feeling, awareness, creativity, and meaning embedded in daily experience. He writes:

> Poetics calls attention to aspects of the natural and human world that express qualities of poetry—that is, of compressed and intensified feeling, awareness, gratitude, and the like. . . . What can be called "a poetics of experience" emphasizes how individuals make sense of, and are influenced by, what they perceive. This process of active response to the world, involving a deepening understanding and sensitivity, mirrors how events, actions, and the conduct of others can all express intellectual, aesthetic, and moral meanings. (Hansen, 2004, p. 122)

In other words, poetics is inherent in the nature of experience itself, and becomes present when the person pays full attention and is fully engaged in experience. Poetics is not the privileged domain of the poet, but belongs to every person fully engaged with the world.

As a witness, Hansen is a humble pilgrim.[3] He bears no will to control or change the world. Instead, he seeks to build an ethical relationship with the world by listening, witnessing, and receiving the world. It is a position of humble reception and critical reflection combined with wonder and love. In my reading of Hansen's work, I find that the invention of the idea of "bearing witness" is a continuous development of his art of self-cultivation and his philosophy of life. From reading his autobiographical essay "On Wonder," as well as from my conversations with him, it is clear that Hansen is not a romantic or utopian thinker. While he is deeply concerned about the human condition, he remains open to the many ways in which "the good" appears amid either the mundane or chaotic features of the world. "Bearing witness" is thus not only an approach to educational research, but also a compelling desire to engage with the world. In my view, the notion implies a fundamental faith in life itself. The task of improving the world must begin with the individual's practice of self-cultivation. The art of self-cultivation is the ethical task of the person dwelling in the world. It is a decentering of one's attention on oneself to the world in which one dwells, to listening, to speaking thoughtfully, and to thinking as best as one can about the meaning of experience. This is the practice of the art of living as an ongoing education (Hansen, 2010a).

When the researcher or educator situates themselves in a humble, appreciative, and reflective position, they become more open to the active, intensive, and creative interchange of energies between self and world. As Dewey remarks, "one of the functions of art is precisely to sap the moralistic timidity that causes the mind to shy away from some materials and refuses to admit them into the clear and purifying light of perceptive consciousness" (Dewey, 1934, p. 189). Similarly, Hansen suggests that "poetics calls attention to aspects of the natural and human world that express qualities of poetry—that is, of compressed and intensified feeling, awareness, gratitude, and the like. . . . [It is] the heightened sense of meaning, artfulness and delight" (Hansen, 2004, p. 122).

Hansen's philosophy of the art of living shares much in common with ideas of life articulated in Chinese philosophy. In this Chinese tradition of the art of living there is also special emphasis placed on practices of self-cultivation, often through reflection on the relationship of the self with the world. Self-cultivation requires patient, continuous, lifelong efforts toward self-perfection in daily life (Chen, 2015). To some extent, classical Chinese poetry is the artistic expression of this philosophical tradition of self-cultivation. This poetry is measured less by literary standards than by its serving as a reflection of the poet's quality as a moral guide, as a person capable of living well and being in harmonious relationship with the universe.

This tradition of the art of self-cultivation, which is embodied mainly in classic Chinese poetry, was cut off radically by the process of China's modernization at the turn of the 20th century. Chinese society experienced dramatic change in almost every respect: political turnover, economic collapse, social chaos. However, the most radical change was cultural. The traditional culture, with its values, customs, and basic beliefs, was utterly negated, mainly by the leadership of the intellectual class associated with radical liberalism. Confucius was the most recognized icon to be overthrown, along with the many cultural legacies associated with his philosophy over the course of 2,000 years. The West, with its related political, cultural, social, and philosophical ideas, became the new authority during the modernization process at the turn of the 20th century (Chow, 1960; Yü-Sheng, 1979).

The risk associated with the closing-off of tradition echoes Hansen's sophisticated elaboration of cosmopolitanism as education. He clearly distinguishes the idea of *tradition* from *traditionalism*. The latter term indicates "a kind of frozen cultural condition—or, better, an attempt to freeze culture as it is," while tradition is "a living, dynamic relation with the past and one's heritage" (Hansen & Zhang, 2017, p. 46). Hansen claims that an appropriate attitude toward tradition is in harmony with a cosmopolitan orientation toward culture: "the capacity to fuse reflective openness to the new with reflective loyalty to the known" (Hansen, 2010b, p. 151). He says that this orientation is also a kind of cultural creativity. To reach this orientation, it is important to witness the very lively and creative interactions between different people and between the individual with their changing environment. This attitude is precious and critically relevant to the ongoing cultural crisis that Chinese society is experiencing.

By being reflectively open to the new (mainly to Western influence, in the case of Chinese modern history) and being reflectively loyal to known (i.e., to the traditional culture of Chinese society built over thousands of years), we need to creatively rebuild the living connection with tradition while re-innovating the tradition within contemporary life, fused with an international perspective. Living in a completely different social context from the past, we could not take tradition as an asset we own but must take it as an evolving one, so that it is possible to creatively build a lively and energetic connection with it. This is precisely the cosmopolitan orientation that Hansen proposes. It is a historical responsibility that contemporary Chinese society faces.

If we consider education as *the* most important means of cultural inheritance and cultural renewal, then the movement of Chinese educational reform needs to pay close attention to the potentiality of creativity and poetics embedded in students' and teachers' daily life experience. Hansen's lifelong study on education as the art of living, his recent invention of "bearing witness" as an approach to the study of teaching and teachers, as well as his philosophical orientation of cosmopolitanism as education, are all closely relevant to the context of Chinese educational reform.

NOTES

1. This poem, titled "Sitting Alone in Face of Mount Jingting," is by the Chinese poet laureate Li Bai (701–762) of the Tang Dynasty (618–907). I have made minor adjustments to the translation. Bai, L. (2014). *Selected poems of Li Bai* (X. Yuanchong, Trans.). China Translation & Publishing Company.

2. My book *John Dewey, Liang Shuming, and China's education reform: Cultivating individuality* (2013) focuses on the question, "How is self-cultivation possible within a radically changing Chinese society?"

3. Pilgrim is also a metaphor Hansen (2017a) uses to describe the idea of "bearing witness."

REFERENCES

Chen, Y. (2015). Pragmatism as an intermediary between Chinese and Marxist philosophy. *Academic Monthly, 47*(7), 5–12.

Chow, T. (1960). *The May Fourth movement: Intellectual revolution in modern China*. Harvard University Press.

Dewey, J. (1931). *Individualism old and new*. George Allen & Unwin.

Dewey, J. (1934). *Art as experience*. Capricorn Books.

Dewey, J. (1984). *John Dewey, the later works 1925–1953: Vol. 2. 1925–1927, Essays, reviews, miscellany, and The public and its problems* (J. A. Boydston, Ed.). Southern Illinois University Press.

Garrison, J. (2001). An introduction to Dewey's theory of functional "trans-action": An alternative paradigm for activity theory. *Mind, Culture, and Activity, 8*(4), 275–296.

Hansen, D. T. (1988). Was Socrates a Socratic teacher? *Educational Theory, 38*(2), 213–224.

Hansen, D. T. (1992). The emergence of shared morality in a classroom. *Curriculum Inquiry, 22*(4), 345–361.

Hansen, D. T. (1993). From role to person: The moral layeredness of classroom teaching. *American Education Research Journal, 30*(4), 651–674.

Hansen, D. T. (2002). Well-formed, not well-filled: Montaigne and the paths of personhood. *Educational Theory, 52*(2), 127–154.

Hansen, D. T. (2004). A poetics of teaching. *Educational Theory, 54*(2), 119–142.

Hansen, D. T. (2005). Creativity in teaching and building a meaningful life as a teacher. *Journal of Aesthetic Education, 39*(2), 57–68.

Hansen, D. T. (2010a). Cosmopolitanism and education: A view from the ground. *Teachers College Record, 112*(1), 1–30.

Hansen, D. T. (2010b). Chasing butterflies without a net: Interpreting cosmopolitanism. *Studies in Philosophy and Education, 29*(2), 151–166.

Hansen, D. T. (2011). *The teacher and the world: A study of cosmopolitanism as education*. Routledge.

Hansen, D. T. (2014). On wonder. In L. J. Waks (Ed.), *Leaders in philosophy of education* (pp. 117–131). Sense Publishers.

Hansen, D. T. (2017a). Among school teachers: Bearing witness as an orientation in educational inquiry. *Educational Theory, 67*(1), 9–30.

Hansen, D. T. (2017b). Bearing witness to teaching and teachers. *Journal of Curriculum Studies, 49*(1), 7–23.

Hansen, D. T. (2018). Bearing witness to the fusion of person and role in teaching. *Journal of Aesthetic Education, 52*(4), 21–48.

Hansen, D. T. & Zhang, H. (2017). Re-imagining educational research on teaching: An interview with Dr. David T. Hansen. In Z. Zhu, A. L. Goodwin, & H. Zhang (Eds.), *Quality of teacher education and learning: Theory and practice* (pp. 35–50). Springer Nature.

Yü-Sheng, L. (1979). *The crisis of Chinese consciousness: Radical antitraditionalism in the May Fourth era*. University of Wisconsin Press.

Zhang, H. (2013). *John Dewey, Liang Shuming, and China's education reform: Cultivating individuality*. Lexington Books.

CHAPTER 6

Dewey, Hansen, and the Moral Heart of Teaching

Ruth Heilbronn

INTRODUCTION

For over 25 years, David Hansen has worked extensively with teachers and teacher educators and has also written much on John Dewey's thought on educational issues.[1] He believes that "Dewey advanced a rich and elevated picture of the teacher's responsibilities" (Hansen, 2007, p. 74), which he draws on in his own work. While some of the discussions of Dewey's work are discrete in individual papers or chapters, their significance comes out most clearly in his two books *The Call to Teach* (1995) and *Exploring the Moral Heart of Teaching* (2001).

Hansen is not alone in acknowledging the influence of Dewey, whose wide-ranging work underpins much philosophy of education. His use of the subtitle *Towards a Teacher's Creed* in his book *Exploring the Moral Heart of Teaching*, together with the book's first chapter, deliberately invokes Dewey's *My Pedagogic Creed* (1972/1897), and this is explicit in a discussion on "the Vitality of Tradition" (Hansen, 2001, p. 8). Hansen draws on a humanistic tradition of education for human flourishing and highlights how Dewey saw something of a similar tension between education as a public service and the pursuit of individual and material aims encouraged by current educational policy. Dewey wrote that learning comes about in the context of shared experience, of doing and experiencing with others, through "joint activity by the use of things" (Dewey, 1916, p. 33). Education needs the conditions for such learning to be possible so as to advance human flourishing. For Dewey and Hansen these conditions have to engage the learner and the teacher within a communal endeavor. Moreover, the humanistic aims of education "need to be as aesthetically and morally rich as circumstance and imagination permit" (Hansen, 2017b, p. xxii).

At the heart of Hansen and Dewey is a belief in education's transformative function:

Education implies growth, which for Dewey means not just "change" with respect to adding discrete skills or bits of information, but transformation in one's very being, however microscopic these metamorphoses will be in most instances. (Hansen, 2017b, p. xxii)

Hansen concentrates on several concepts and ideas that are particularly relevant to his own work as a teacher and teacher educator, and to his effort to understand and articulate what makes a good teacher. His interest is in the human being who inhabits the role of the teacher, and what the teacher must do to flourish in the role.

Good teaching requires a continuously developing sense of judgment regarding how to engage students in subject matter, how to interpret their understanding, how to draw upon their experience to help them perceive the significance of their studies, how to cultivate a supportive learning community in the class-room, and much more. (Hansen, 2017a, p. 8)

I turn now to discuss four key Deweyan ideas that are notable in Hansen's writing—first, habit and growth; second, context and situation; third, moral knowledge; and lastly, democracy as shared living. However, when reading Dewey, we ought to be mindful that his work is an organic whole in that the concepts he employs are often interrelated and linked in a nexus of complementary concepts, which is very much a function of his naturalizing philosophy. It is a mistake to isolate one concept from its place in this web of interconnected ideas.

HABIT AND GROWTH

Hansen stresses the importance of habits in education—particularly in rela-tion to upholding the values of liberal education, with openness and toler-ance of democratic values at its heart. He tells us that "democratic habits remain as vital for education and culture today as they were when Dewey published *Democracy and Education* in 1916" (Hansen & James, 2016, p. 94). Habits are built up through experience:

A person can continuously refine and reform habits that trigger, in turn, a more efficacious and expansive response to new experience. This process of refinement and reconstruction constitutes the ideal spiral of growth that we see as informing Dewey's educational philosophy in *Democracy and Education*. (Hansen & James, 2016, p. 94)

Growth is a key concept for Dewey (Keall, 2010; Bernstein, 2010, p. 92; Heilbronn, 2017). The fourth chapter of *Democracy and Education* begins with a statement regarding the interrelationship between society and the child, the role of education and the idea of growth. Dewey tells us that "in directing the activities of the young, society determines its own future" (Dewey, 1916, p. 46). Children's development relies on mutual dependency in the sense that the young experience and experiment within their social milieu, and they receive the culture and mediated experience of adults. This is how society develops. Key qualities that enable this development are flexibility and plasticity. With their social responsiveness, children learn from experience and develop dispositions and habits. Active adjustments to the environment develop into "habits of active use of our surroundings" (Dewey, 1916, p. 52).

For Hansen, as for Dewey, this plasticity enables the power to develop dispositions (Hansen & James, 2016, p. 98), and in this development another key Deweyan concept is introduced, that of intelligence. "Intelligence marks the disposition to observe, to take note, to reflect and to respond" (Hansen & James, p. 98). Since habits can be mechanical or dynamic, "to carry habits means to embody them intelligently" (Hansen & James, p. 98). Intelligence "comes into play in responsiveness, the ability to reflect. Moreover, dynamic habits are flexible and embodied. . . . They support the pursuit of ends-in-view, as Dewey conceives this term" (Hansen & James, p. 95).

Hansen's understanding draws on a close reading of Dewey, a deep experience of classrooms, and many hours of conversations with teachers. Hansen can therefore illustrate the notion of growth from experience through direct observation of a teacher who asks a shy student, previously not participating in class, to read a passage from their text out loud.

> Instantly, the teacher has attained her end-in-view: the student has just participated. In that same instant, the student's participation becomes a method. That is, knowing now that the student has spoken, the teacher will deploy that fact as a means. She can now ask the student to comment on what they've read—which instantly constitutes the attainment of her next end-in-view, namely an ascent in the terms of the student's participation. That step, in turn, becomes a means to further growth. It is growth for both the student, who step by step comes further into the ethos of dialogue, and it is growth for the teacher, who has learned how to support the student and may, as a consequence, now have a wider perspective on how to support others in the class. (Hansen & James, 2016, p. 95)

The illustration continues by revealing how the student has in the eyes of classmates transformed into "a new student," as one who participates in class. The teacher has performed a critical educational role in the life of the classroom, because they have created conditions for the students

> to literally form or constitute the selves they are—for example, to transform from a withdrawn individual into a publicly expressive one. At the same time,

the teacher can encourage her students (and herself) not to regard one another as "fixed" personalities with "fixed" identities—the "good" student, the "row-dy" one, the "A" student, the goody-two-shoes, the brooder, the class clown. Classroom settings can become downright tyrannical if participants fail to grant one another the right to grow. (Hansen & James, 2016, p. 95)

Here we have a process-based explanation involving growth, transfor-mation, and a community of learners. Hansen explains how this process has been described by Dewey in *Democracy and Education* in that Dewey cap-tures the teacher's ongoing conduct in remarking that habits are "tendencies to respond in certain ways to change in the environment so as to bring about other changes" (Hansen & James, 2016, p. 95). A good teacher "by and through her habits, is constantly on the lookout for educative possibilities" (Hansen & James, p. 95). And the process is iterative, since

> Once the teacher and student begin to reflect on their experience—ideally, together—they position themselves to keep their evolving habits of engagement open and responsive. In this way, the rhythmic play of ends and means illumi-nates the dynamic structure of habit that underlies it. Dynamic habits contrast with routinized habits and externally imposed, fixed ends. (Hansen & James, 2016, p. 95)

In his commentary on this classroom occurrence, Hansen notes that people can continuously refine and reform habits, which can then trigger "a more efficacious and expansive response to new experience" (Hansen & James, 2016, p. 95). He calls this process of refinement and reconstruction "the ideal spiral of growth" and comments that this "spiral of growth" in-forms Dewey's entire educational philosophy. From Dewey's account of habits Hansen concludes that people "can learn—or fail to learn—how to cultivate habits that are truly responsive to experience in all its intellectual, aesthetic and somatic complexity" (Hansen & James, p. 96), and he directs us to Dewey's account of plasticity in *Democracy and Education* to explain the capacity of a human being to acquire "a habit of learning," through which one "learns to learn" in the encounter with the new. As Dewey states:

> Habits take the form both of habituation, or a general and persistent balance of organic activities with the surroundings, and of active capacities to readjust activity to meet new conditions. (Dewey, 1916, p. 57)

Dewey's discussion of habit in relation to growth is key for Hansen's philosophy of education. Hansen writes:

> Dewey dissolves the stereotypical notion that habits refer solely to mechanical, repetitive and mindless routines. . . . He reconstructs the concept so that we can

see why habits can become both stable and dynamic: they can evolve through action and reflection upon the consequences of action. (Hansen & James, 2016, p. 97)

The evolving nature of habits, and our reflection on them, becomes significant to the work that good teachers do with their students and good teacher educators do with teachers in formation.

THE SITUATION

The story analyzed above points to the importance of the situation in which learning takes place, echoing a familiar refrain from Dewey concerning the fact of humans' social embeddedness. Elsewhere, Hansen offers examples that illustrate how the concept of situation can illuminate the richness of classroom life and augment our understanding of pedagogical moments:

One morning a student in my second period history class asks me a question about the document we're studying, and I move to respond to her. We have simultaneously created and entered a situation. . . . The "we," however, includes more than the student and me. It includes every other student who has overheard the question, it includes the question, it includes the document, it includes whatever transpired right before the posing of the question that in one way or another created the very possibility of the action, it includes the circumstances that have licensed the student to speak and me to listen, and much, much more. It includes the student's prior learning as a student of history, as a student in my classroom, as a student in this school and, once more, the list goes on. (Hansen & James, 2016, p. 99)

And, again, Hansen plays on this Deweyan theme by underscoring the fact of our temporal embeddedness in learning situations:

We cannot live in the past or future. In the present moment, we can project a future—for example, an upcoming essay assignment and how the study of the historical document figures into it. In that same moment, we can draw upon the past—our memories of a previous discussion of a similar kind of text. Nonetheless, all projecting and all remembrance take form in the present moment. (Hansen & James, 2016, pp. 100–101)

Thus, "the situation" is a way of referring to the context and everything within the context, such as others who participate in our experience and physical settings. In this sense, Dewey also uses the term *environment* as analogous to *situation*. Arguably, this would serve as an example of the kind of ambiguity found in some of Dewey's concepts often identified by commentators. However, Hansen, as a sympathetic reader of Dewey, is able to see through to the underlying connections of Dewey's ideas and their implications for educational practice. He avoids harping on analytical concerns in his use of Dewey, especially where these are not relevant to the underlying significance of Dewey's ideas. As a case in point, Hansen reveals how the Deweyan idea of the environment can give shape to our habits, which, in turn, influences how we teach indirectly through the environment:

> These environments call out of us particular emotions, thoughts, actions, responses, all of which can be educative—if the environment is constructed with care and foresight—or miseducative if the environment has been neglected. . . . The environment, in short, influences our habit formation. (Hansen & James, 2016, pp. 100–101)

In an earlier article, Hansen (2002) examines in more detail what he describes as "the main contours of John Dewey's conception of environment for teaching and learning" (Hansen, p. 267), analyzing how Dewey's conception of the environment derives from two components of his philosophical anthropology—the first being his understanding of the nature of a growing self, and the second his view of how human beings influence one another. The article discusses why Dewey argues that an environment for teaching and learning should be what he calls "simplified, purified, balanced, and steadying" (Hansen, p. 272). And further, Hansen shows how Dewey distinguishes an educative environment from what he calls "surroundings." This analysis leads in the final section of the article to a conclusion with direct application to teachers, one that chimes along with the current critique of what Biesta (2015) calls "the learnification of education." Hansen uses this analysis to urge teachers not to focus directly on learning but rather on the environment that obtains in the classroom. Indeed, he tells us "how timely and powerful Dewey's conception of an environment remains for teachers, teacher educators, and all who care about meaningful teaching" (Hansen, 2002, p. 267).

MORAL KNOWLEDGE, TEACHERS, AND CURRICULUM

Hansen has written widely on teachers and their ethical roles and responsibilities in the context of what he terms *moral knowledge*. To get at what is meant it is useful to first look at how Dewey conceives of "knowledge." Dewey held that the traditional use of the term knowledge commits "the great intellectualist fallacy" (Dewey, 1984/1929, p. 232), and he believed that if we draw our conception of knowledge from reflection on actual conditions of science and life, instead of from the prejudices of history, we would understand that there is no genuine split between theory and practice.

This view of knowledge is significant for Hansen's work with teachers and his understanding of how moral knowledge pertains to the work of teaching. Hansen's views on moral knowledge convey the importance of reflective activity in teaching as a rational reflection on what is experienced in practice. His writing on the subject reminds us specifically of Dewey's pragmatic view of knowledge and how this view leads to an understanding of the teacher's role as a fundamentally ethical one. The intellectual and moral aspects of any experience cannot be isolated, just as knowledge itself is an integration between the knower and the known.

> What is learned and employed in an occupation having an aim and involving cooperation with others is moral knowledge, whether consciously so regarded or not. For it builds up a social interest and confers the intelligence needed to make that interest effective in practice. (Dewey, 1916, p. 366)

Teaching a particular curriculum engages students with both an intellectual and a moral content that cannot stand apart. Dewey states that the subjects of the curriculum are "organs of initiation into social values" (Dewey, 1916, p. 367). And further, that when,

> [a]cquired under conditions where their social significance is realized, they feed moral interest and develop moral insight. Moreover, the qualities of mind discussed under the topic of method of learning are all of them intrinsically moral qualities. Open-mindedness, single-mindedness, sincerity, breadth of outlook, thoroughness, assumption of responsibility for developing the consequences of ideas which are accepted, are moral traits. (Dewey, 1916, p. 367)

For Hansen, as for Dewey, the school curriculum carries moral knowledge, in the way it is taught, and in the experience of sharing a classroom conversation through questioning and reflecting. The detailed narratives and analyses that create the four case studies that Hansen puts together in *The Call to Teach* bring this out clearly. Hansen puts forward a view of the curriculum in which there is a moral dimension to whatever is taught, no matter the circumstances. One of the numerous examples he offers in *The Call to Teach* illustrates this. Ms. Payton struggles to adapt her curriculum to her students and finds that the endeavor engages her in difficult emotions, as when she realizes from her reflections that she has at times been mean to students who are struggling. This leads her into an understanding of what needs to change if she is to enable all her students to access the curriculum:

> [It] covers the feeling of accepting people. I mean that I think it's morally wrong to demand of someone that which they cannot accomplish. . . . I think we have to do more than just say the curriculum that we're offering students is the right curriculum. (Hansen, 1995, p. 36)

Hansen points us to the context in which teaching takes place to explain that the process of reflection and change "invariably takes time and steadfastness, both of which she was willing to invest" (Hansen, 1995, p. 36).

In such observations, Hansen echoes Dewey's view that "the moral purpose of the school is universal and dominant in all instruction, whatever the topic" (Dewey, 1909, p. 2). In detailing the nuanced narratives of classroom life in *The Call to Teach*, Hansen illustrates how this learning comes about. Dewey is explicit on this matter and believes that all subjects should be taught in a way so as to bring out the social and cultural implications of the curriculum and relate them to the experience of students. An example of Dewey's considers the teaching of geography, about which he writes that "the ultimate significance of lake, river, mountain, and plain is not physical but social; it is the part which it plays in modifying and directing human relationships" (Dewey, p. 35). Recognizing such moral principles is to recognize the morality inherent to learning, which always consists in the relation of the individual to the social. Teachers, in Dewey's view, need to possess subject-matter knowledge, but they also must take into account how the content that they are teaching relates socially, and particularly to the lives of students:

> [F]inding the material for learning within experience is only the first step. The next step is the progressive development of what is already experienced into a fuller and richer and also more organized form, a form that gradually approximates that in which subject-matter is presented to the skilled, mature person. (Dewey, 1988, p. 48)

Every occasion in school is a potential exploration of the terrain of ethics education, and in this, teaching subject matter is no different from other activities experienced by students. As Hansen affirms, "all knowledge becomes moral in meaning and consequence when deployed in situations where people heed the concerns, interests, questions and aspirations of others alongside their own" (Hansen, 2007, p. 180).

DEMOCRACY AND SHARED LIVING

The discussion above on ethics and curriculum takes us now to a fourth area where Dewey has influenced Hansen, particularly in his emphasis on moral education for democratic living. Dewey views collaborative processes as essential to any learning:

> Since a democratic society repudiates the principle of external authority, it must find a substitute in voluntary disposition and interest; these can be created only by education. But there is a deeper explanation. A democracy is more than a

form of government; it is primarily a mode of associated living, of conjoint communicated experience. (Dewey, 1916, p. 57)

Dewey put his faith in a democratic system of government, but his writings do not defend the claim to democracy merely as a preferred system of government. Defining democracy as a form of associated living makes a limited claim. What is at stake is a belief in deliberative processes to drive educational practices. The normative aspect is embodied in a belief in the rationality and morality of these deliberative processes that, in themselves, constitute a way to ensure growth and development. There is a long way between the concept of deliberative participation and democracy as a system of government. There is a chasm between these two notions that is not bridged in Dewey's work, which has led to the accusation that Dewey is naively optimistic in his belief in progressive development (Rockefeller, 1991; Boisevert, 1999).[2]

For Dewey, the school is a place with a fundamental moral purpose relating to inducting children into the life of society and preparing them to take their place in the world. The school is an institution erected by society to contribute to "maintaining the life and advancing the welfare of society" (Dewey, 1909, p. 7), and crucially, "we must take the child as a member of society in the broadest sense, and demand for and from the schools whatever is necessary to enable the child intelligently to recognize all his social relations and take his part in sustaining them" (Dewey, p. 9). In Dewey's philosophy, the child is "an organic whole, intellectually, socially and morally, as well as physically" (Dewey, p. 9). This rich view of the child entails an ethical responsibility on the school to provide an education that will give the child "such possession of himself that he may take charge of himself" and in so doing have power to shape and direct social changes (Dewey, p. 11).

Dewey's central tenet in his *Moral Principles in Education* is that, "Only as we interpret school activities with reference to the larger circle of social activities to which they relate do we find any standard for judging their moral significance" (Dewey, 1909, p. 13). We find strong echoes of this in Hansen's work; for example, the whole project of *The Call to Teach* expresses a commitment to education as a public service:

Teachers teach not to serve themselves but rather to serve others, students first and foremost but by extension the communities and the society in which they live. Moreover, teaching implies serving learners in ways that are distinct from those of other practices. (Hansen, 1995, p. 140)

Further, he deems it important for teachers to develop dispositions that dispose them "to move into, rather than out of, the social and moral complexity of dwelling in genuine community with other people" (Hansen, 2001, p. 60).

> Democratic habits dispose a person to look outwards with care and persistence on the public scene. These habits give a person courage to act, rather than merely to spectate. They lead a person to respond to the presence of other people, with their diverse views and orientations, rather than to withdraw from them. As we interpret Dewey, he regards what we are calling dynamic, democratic habits as potentially informing the very substance of the self, a self that constitutes itself through action and reflection upon action. (Hansen, 2007, p. 96)

Like Dewey, Hansen expresses his deep adherence to democratic values and the importance of developing democratic habits through education.

CONCLUSION

Dewey's work has drawn much criticism, particularly from analytic philosophers (Peters, 1977), who have deplored the lack of clarity of some of his definitions, such as purported shortcomings in his views of democracy (Flew, 1977; Whipple, 2005), his theories of knowledge and inquiry (Quinton, 1977), and the implications of his views on growth for curriculum implementation (Wright Mills, 1966; Hirsch, 1987; Ravitch, 2000). It is difficult to find critique of this kind in the work of David Hansen. I believe this to be the result of Hansen's' primary ontological commitment to teachers and teaching, to explicating "the moral heart of teaching" and to standing in solidarity with teachers. His scholarship on Dewey is extensive: It is in some sense a partisan scholarship, drawn on to illuminate his life's commitment to supporting and developing teachers and their existential stance in the classroom. It is an engaged philosophy of education that does not seek to dispassionately examine Dewey's ideas, but to draw on them as a source of illumination. In this spirit, the concluding section suggests three aspects of Hansen's work that have implications for educational practice—first, the impact of digital technologies; second, the importance of engagement in the public domain; and third, a commitment to standing in solidarity with teachers.

Digital Technologies

Contemporary educational practices need to take account of digital technologies due to the issues and controversies their use engenders. Questions arise for educators around the potential dangers to social life in a networked era and how living in a technologically mediated world might impact education and culture. Simultaneously, teachers also look to how digital technologies might support educational developments. Hansen relates technical knowhow with social consciousness (2007) and suggests that when this perspective is applied, educators have a way into the educative uses of technology.

Hansen and James (2016) direct us to Dewey for guidance on technology in educational settings, through understanding that the moral aspects of any learning situation are inseparable from purely technical aspects. When tools are used in the interests of a truly shared life, such appliances become the positive resources of civilization. As Hansen highlights, like any other curricular area, teachers need to apply a moral and critical stance to using digital technologies.

Taking a Stance

Hansen's published work in support of teachers and humanistic teacher education puts him, like Dewey, in the realm of the public intellectual. Drawing on Dewey's 1927 book *The Public and its Problems,* Hansen states that "For Dewey a truly 'civil civilization' features social responsibility, commitments, and open communication" (Hansen, 2007, p. 179). He reminds us how Dewey regrets the divorce of knowledge from social consequences in public and private ethos and calls attention to the damaging consequences of the gulf between humanities and natural sciences due to an alleged split between "mind and spirit." "Polarization of knowledge divided against itself mirrors the polarization from one another of all too many individuals and communities in society" (Hansen, p. 179). In defending teacher education and the critical role of teachers, Hansen takes a stance through his published work and in his teaching. Hansen embodies Dewey's ideas that "through communication we convert the event into a meaning, into a moment that can educate and urge us to move onwards" (Hansen, 2004, p. 22).

Solidarity with Teachers

Hansen offers a challenge to the educator to engage in practice that exemplifies solidarity with teachers and students alike. In the current climate of performativity this reminds us that what is sustaining and renewing for teachers and students is to cultivate habits of intellectual focus, curiosity, and a readiness to engage the new. Dispositions such as these can help to arm teachers in uncertain times. Educators have an ethical responsibility to not mislead those they teach, and in the case of teacher educators, to not misrepresent or ignore the tensions and difficulties of the practice, in order to prepare future teachers "to understand the moral and ethical complexities of their role and thus enable them to reflect ethical actions and decisions in their professional practice" (Campbell, 1997, 255). Hansen reminds us of the qualities that must be developed and in this indicates how he stands by teachers in their endeavors:

> [T]eaching requires a continuously developing sense of judgment regarding how to engage students in subject matter, how to interpret their understanding, how

to draw upon their experience to help them perceive the significance of their studies, how to cultivate a supportive learning community in the classroom, and much more. . . . The moral baseline in the present article is the view that teachers are singular persons who, with the right support, bring commitment, knowledge, a sympathetic outlook, and other human offerings to their work with the young. (Hansen, 2017a, p. 8)

This support is vital because teachers' practice "inevitably has a strong influence on the moral lessons students directly and indirectly acquire in the classroom" (Campbell, 1997, p. 255). Teachers need support as they have a heavy responsibility to be ethical in their practice. The ethical responsibility to those taught is an ethic of solidarity with them. This is how I interpret Hansen's work for and with teachers, many of whom work in difficult conditions, and whose values often conflict with those of their school and colleagues. In his philosophical writings drawing on Dewey, and in bearing witness to teachers in their existential stance, David Hansen gives a strong account of education that has at its core "the moral heart of teaching."

NOTES

1. Other philosophers whom Hansen has studied extensively and applied in his educational work are Plato, Michel de Montaigne, Sor Juana Inés de la Cruz.
2. Saito (2005) attempts to ward off such critiques in her reading of Dewey through a lens of Emersonian "moral perfectionism." It is an interesting account that highlights the "glimmer of light" in Dewey's abiding faith in democracy. Saito establishes that Dewey's project is one of hope for the future, to be achieved through education.

REFERENCES

Bernstein, R. J. (2010). *The pragmatic turn*. Polity Press.
Biesta, G. (2015). What is education good for? On good education, teacher judgement, and educational professionalism. *European Journal of Education, 50*(1), 75–87.
Boisvert, R. D. (1999). The nemesis of necessity: Tragedy's challenge to Deweyan pragmatism. In C. Haskins & D. I. Seiple (Eds.), *Dewey reconfigured: Essays on Deweyan pragmatism* (pp. 151–168). State University of New York Press.
Campbell, E. (1997). Connecting the ethics of teaching and moral education. *Journal of Teacher Education, 48*(4), 255–263.
Dewey, J. (1909). *Moral principles in education*. Houghton Mifflin Company.
Dewey, J. (1916). *Democracy and education*. Macmillan Company.
Dewey, J. (1972). My pedagogic creed. In *The early works of John Dewey, 1882–1898. Vol. 5. 1895–1898, Early essays* (J. A. Boydston, Ed.). Southern Illinois University Press. (Original work published 1897)

Dewey, J. (1984). *John Dewey, the later works 1925–1953: Vol. 4. 1929, The quest for certainty* (J. A. Boydston, Ed.). Southern Illinois University Press. (Original work published 1929)

Dewey, J. (1988). *John Dewey, the later works 1925–1953: Vol. 13 1938–1939, Experience and education, Freedom and culture, Theory of valuation, and essays* (J. A. Boydston, Ed.). Southern Illinois University Press.

Flew, A. (1977). Democracy and education. In R. S. Peters (Ed.), *John Dewey reconsidered* (pp. 48–65). Routledge & Kegan Paul.

Hansen, D. T. (1995). *The call to teach*. Teachers College Press.

Hansen, D. T. (2001). *Exploring the moral heart of teaching: Toward a teacher's creed*. Teachers College Press.

Hansen, D. T. (2002). Dewey's conception of an environment for teaching and learning. *Curriculum Inquiry, 32*(3), 267–280.

Hansen, D. T. (2004). John Dewey's call for meaning. *Education and Culture, 20*(2), 7–24.

Hansen, D. T. (2007). John Dewey and a curriculum of moral knowledge. *Curriculum and Teaching Dialogue, 9*(1–2), 173–181.

Hansen, D. T. (2017a). Bearing witness to teaching and teachers. *Journal of Curriculum Studies, 49*(1), 7–23.

Hansen, D. T. (2017b). Foreword. In L. Waks & A. English (Eds.), *John Dewey's Democracy and education: A centennial handbook*. Cambridge University Press.

Hansen, D. T. & James, C. (2016). The importance of cultivating democratic habits in schools: Enduring lessons from *Democracy and Education*. *Journal of Curriculum Studies, 48*(1), 94–112.

Heilbronn, R. (2017). Dewey and culture: Responding to "extreme views." *Journal of Philosophy of Education, 51*(1), 89–101.

Hirsch, Jr., E. D. (1987). *Cultural literacy: What every American needs to know*. Houghton Mifflin.

Keall, C. (2010). Exploring the nature and educational significance of Dewey's notion of growth. In *Panel: The centrality of Dewey's philosophy of growth: Clarifying Dewey's commitment to growth in ethics and education*. Society for the Advancement of American Philosophy, 37th Annual Meeting, University of North Carolina.

Peters, R. S. (Ed.). (1977). *John Dewey reconsidered*. Routledge & Kegan Paul.

Quinton, A. (1977). John Dewey's theory of knowledge. In R. S. Peters (Ed.), *John Dewey reconsidered* (pp. 1–12). Routledge & Kegan Paul.

Ravitch, D. (2000). *Left Back: A century of battles over school reform*. Simon & Schuster.

Rockefeller, S. (1991). *John Dewey: Religious faith and democratic humanism*. Columbia University Press.

Saito, N. (2005). *The gleam of light: Moral perfectionism and education in Dewey and Emerson*. Fordham University Press.

Whipple, M. (2005). The Dewey-Lippmann debate today: Communication distortions, reflective agency, and participatory democracy. *Sociology Today, 23*(1), 156–178.

Wright Mills, C. (1966). *Sociology and pragmatism: The higher learning in America*. Paine-Whitman.

CHAPTER 7

Tradition, Teaching, and the Play of Influence

Pádraig Hogan

FROM A SENSE OF TRADITION TO TEACHING AS A TRADITION

David Hansen's ongoing researches have yielded a wealth of insights into the importance of tradition for teaching as a human occupation. I find Hansen's explorations fertile and illuminating, not least because they are characteristically informed by perceptive reflections on the educational contexts in which he has worked as a teacher, both in schools and universities. This critical spotlight on educational experience, moreover, gives Hansen's arguments a pedagogical incisiveness and revelatory power. In fact, there is little in Hansen's work that I would wish, in the accustomed manner of academic philosophy, to confront or seek to refute. There are many themes, however, that I would wish to engage with, converse about, and seek to explore further. Tradition and its educational import is one such theme. The notion of tradition itself is rather vast, so it may be helpful to focus here on some of Hansen's key thoughts on tradition in education, as presented and developed in three of his books over a quarter-century. In this opening part of the chapter, I will try to summarize some of Hansen's distinctive arguments on tradition in education and identify a few points for further investigation. In the second part, I will seek to examine two differing conceptions of tradition, and I will then in the third part offer some further remarks on teaching as a distinct tradition in its own right.

In his 1995 book *The Call to Teach*, Hansen explored teaching as a vocation, or an unforced "summons or bidding to be of service" (Hansen, p. 1). While not excluding the self-denial long associated with the word *vocation*, particularly a religious vocation, Hansen placed the main emphasis on more venturesome human qualities that make teaching a particular kind of vocation—being active, creative, engaged, outward-looking, imaginative. The qualities he stresses are, moreover, ones that sustain practitioners in circumstances that can often be unforgiving, or in institutions that can be regularly frustrating. Later in the book Hansen suggests that teaching as a vocation can be enhanced where teachers share "a sense of history and of tradition." And he adds: "If one conceives of oneself as working in a practice whose origins reside far in the past and whose value will persist long into the future, one can derive additional sources of strength and perhaps even of imagination as a teacher" (Hansen, p. 133). He stresses here the importance of sustaining teachers in their work: "The sense of history and tradition in teaching can help teachers place their immediate circumstances against a larger backdrop, one that adds significance to what they perform" (Hansen, p. 135).

In *Exploring the Moral Heart of Teaching*, Hansen (2001) enlarges and refines his thinking on a *sense* of tradition, but also introduces the idea of teaching itself as a *living tradition*. In relation to the former, he stresses a need for teachers—both experienced teachers and student teachers—to cultivate a sense of tradition among themselves, and he identifies two important fruits of this cultivation:

> A sense of tradition generates for the teacher a critical distance from contemporary conceptions of what teaching is supposedly about. At the same time, it spurs the teacher to engage in self-scrutiny and to keep in view the question of what it means to be a teacher in the first place. (Hansen, 2001, p. 7)

At first sight it may seem strange to associate critical distance and self-scrutiny with a sense of tradition. Having a strong sense of tradition is more usually associated with conservative leanings and with reluctance to call into question the long-settled tenor of things. But a sense of tradition, Hansen argues, is not the same as traditionalism, and here is where the notion of a "living tradition" enters the picture. A living tradition, he continues, "presupposes a community of practitioners, of men and women who, through the generations, have perceived themselves as teachers and who have sought to enact the terms of the work" (Hansen, 2001, p. 116). A living tradition, moreover, "undergoes more or less constant modification and adjustment," especially through ongoing discussions among the practitioners about how their commitments might best be understood and realized. A living tradition would thus be at once a source of pride and an ever-developing challenge; pride in what generations of teachers have contributed to personal and social well-being, and a willingness to embrace the fresh challenges of doing so in the present and the future. As Hansen concludes:

> In a living tradition, practitioners simply do not sail with the prevailing wind. Instead they chart a course that takes them toward the highest possibilities embedded in their practice. They cannot chart that course from nowhere. They need tradition. A practice and a tradition go hand-in-hand. (Hansen, 2001, p. 117)

Linking practice with tradition in this way makes tradition a source not only of virtues but also of fresh inspirations for practitioners. Such a linking lies at the heart of Alasdair MacIntyre's most well-known book, *After Virtue* (1985), and Hansen draws profitably on some of MacIntyre's core arguments in pursuing his own exploration. Briefly, these include: "the narrative unity" in one's life and actions (or the absence of such unity) (MacIntyre, p. 31); the actions that distinguish a practice from other forms of activity (p. 117); the tendency of institutions to privilege the external rewards of a practice (e.g., money, social prestige, reputation) over the inherent goods of a practice (p. 118); "the virtue of having an adequate sense of the traditions to which one belongs" (p. 124). Practitioners—not workers, or employees, or indeed professionals—become central in this account of things.

To argue thus not only highlights the distinctiveness of practice from other forms of work or labor; it also lays claim to a substantial measure of autonomy for anything called a practice. Where teaching is concerned, for example, it implies that this pursuit would be regarded first and foremost as "a purposeful endeavor in its own right" (p. 117), as distinct from a subordinate endeavor to be steered by church, state, or any "ism." It would mean that the self-understanding of teachers would be informed more by internal than external sources. In Hansen's words, teachers would "appreciate that their work has meaning in its own right, rather than solely because it is a socially sanctioned activity or because it leads to socially approved outcomes" (p. 156). This would, moreover, allow teachers "to weigh the various claims they hear about [their] work and to measure them against what the practice itself has bequeathed to them" (p. 126).

In Hansen's later book *The Teacher and the World: A Study of Cosmopolitanism and Education* (2011), the notion of teaching as an autonomous or semiautonomous tradition appears again, but more as a background, or context, than as an explicit theme. To explain what I mean by this, it is necessary to quote an extended passage from the opening pages of the book. Here Hansen raises six questions that link the inquiry he is about to undertake to his earlier ones and that orient the reader to what follows. For ease of reference I have numbered each of the questions in the passage.

(1) What does it mean to be a teacher in a globalised world? (2) Are teachers the hand-servants of the particular state or nation in which they reside? (3) Are they paid functionaries carrying out the dictates of inward-looking authorities? (4) Are they representatives of what might be called the "republic of education" that reaches across political borders and that regards the endeavour as something more than the maintenance of particularistic or nationalistic values? (5) Are teachers charged by the very meaning of education to develop broad, deep, and rich understandings of self, community, and world? (6) What would it mean to be a teacher who grasps and can convey the value of being open reflectively to new ideas, purposes, and people, while also being loyal reflectively to particular beliefs, traditions, and practices?

The first and last questions here are open-ended ones, and the main body of *The Teacher and the World* pursues these in an illuminating way. But in doing so it also presupposes that the answer to the second and third questions is "no" and that the answer to the fourth and fifth questions is "yes." In other words, it assumes that teachers are *not* handservants of the state or nation and that they are *not* paid functionaries. Likewise, it assumes that teachers *are* representatives of something like a "republic of education" and that they *are* called on to uphold and share with their students the inherent values of such a "republic." Hansen succinctly captures the heart of the matter in his six questions. The negative answers presupposed for the second and third questions, and the affirmative answers presupposed for the fourth and fifth, provide decisive orientations for one of the book's main goals: "contributing to an ever-evolving and yet substantive cosmopolitan canon for research, teaching and teacher education" (Hansen, 2011, p. 96). From older times he includes in this canon voices like Socrates, Confucius, Plato, Erasmus, and Montaigne. More recent figures included are Hannah Arendt, W. E. B. Du Bois, Sigmund Freud, George Orwell, Susan Sontag, Rabindranath Tagore, Virginia Woolf, John Dewey, and others. As well as texts, moreover, the canon would include musical works, paintings, and other creations that teachers might come to revere "in the familiar way that certain poems, novels, songs, and sayings become beloved and life-guiding to people" (Hansen, p. 96).

I agree with the answers presupposed for the four "yes/no" questions, but I fear that many would not. For instance, a critic might reasonably claim that any perusal of the history of Western education shows that teachers were predominantly handservants and functionaries through the long course of that history. The critic might even conclude that this control from above has long been the common order of things, and that this remains the case in the dominant tenor of international educational reforms of recent decades. As evidence, the critic might cite the increasing recasting of teaching as work that can be digitally tracked for purposes of comparative ranking, or purposes of reward, remediation, or penalty.

The critic's case is a formidable one, so there is more work that needs to be done before one can conclude—as I would wish to do with Hansen—that teachers are rightly to be regarded as independent practitioners, informed and sustained by a rich and authoritative tradition of educational wisdom. In tackling this work, an ingrained twofold idea needs to be explicitly identified and dislodged: viz. that education is a subordinate vehicle of the party in power, and that teachers are functionaries. This idea needs to be exposed as a disfigurement of education itself as a defensible and promising human undertaking. Here one might begin to uncover an *inescapable* significance of tradition for education. To this task let us now turn.

INVESTIGATING TRADITION: FROM PREFERRED
INHERITANCES TO THE PLAY OF INFLUENCE

The history of philosophy is replete with debates and conflicts between different traditions that have sought conclusive answers to the ultimate questions that arise for human beings. Many traditions in philosophy came to be regarded as "isms"—idealism, realism, empiricism, rationalism, Marxism, utilitarianism, positivism, pragmatism, liberalism, postmodernism, and so on. But in the later 20th century, the notion of tradition itself became an explicit theme for philosophical investigation. Two such investigations are directly pertinent to our inquiry here because they focus on what is inescapable in tradition and help to bring the educational dimensions of tradition into sharper relief. The first investigation is Hans-Georg Gadamer's, undertaken mainly in his *Truth and Method* (Gadamer, 1989), but also in his subsequent writings. The second investigation is Alasdair MacIntyre's, pursued mainly in his trilogy *After Virtue* (1985), *Whose Justice? Which Rationality?* (1988), and *Three Rival Versions of Moral Enquiry* (1999).

TRADITION IN GADAMER'S WRITINGS

Beginning with Gadamer, the "rehabilitation of authority and tradition" that he carried through in the second part of *Truth and Method* cast him as a conservative in the view of many critics (e.g., Habermas, initially and influentially; Derrida; Caputo). In the foreword to the second edition of *Truth and Method*, Gadamer replied that his researches were not concerned with providing support for one or other cause or commitment. He identified his primary concern as bringing to light some truths that have to be acknowledged as undeniable if the nature of human understanding itself is to be properly understood: "My real concern was and is philosophic: not what we do or what we ought to do, but what happens to us above our wanting and doing" (Gadamer, 1989, p. xxviii). This point needs to be stressed because, on a first perusal, Gadamer's account of how human understanding occurs seems to discard epistemology in favor of something like the stance of a traditionalist, or even a controversialist. Here are a few examples: "It is the tyranny of hidden prejudices that makes us deaf to the language that speaks to us in tradition" (Gadamer, p. 270); "all understanding inevitably involves some prejudices" (Gadamer, p. 270); "the prejudices of the individual, far more than his judgements, constitute the historical reality of his being" (Gadamer, pp. 276–277). This last statement, far from being an unconsidered remark, receives emphasis in the German text. It is one of the most representative remarks of Gadamer's philosophy as a whole. A prejudice, Gadamer explains, is "a judgement that is rendered before all the elements that determine a situation have been finally examined" (Gadamer, p. 270). Some prejudices, moreover, could predispose people in open-minded ways as distinct from chauvinistic or acrimonious ways. The Enlightenment, Gadamer argues, gave the notion of prejudice a bad name, displacing its older connotations and associating it essentially with invidious biases and unfounded judgments. Such shortcomings, on the Enlightenment's view of reason, were ingrained in long-established traditions—religious, political, military, cultural—and they had to be replaced by reason, the supreme arbiter in all serious matters of debate.

The point at issue here, and in particular its educational import, becomes clearer if we compare Gadamer's position with that of Thomas Jefferson, a key figure of the Enlightenment in America. When making plans in the early 1820s for a new kind of educational institution, to be called the University of Virginia, Jefferson confidently wrote in a letter to historian William Roscoe: "[T]his institution will be based on the illimitable freedom of the human mind, for here we are not afraid to follow truth wherever it may lead, nor to tolerate any error so long as reason is left free to combat it" (see https://www.monticello.org/site/research-and-collections/follow-truth-quotation).

Jefferson himself had a rich appreciation of inheritances of learning, but he also shared the Enlightenment's inflated beliefs in the powers of reason. The self-assured claims of an Enlightenment conception of reason—to unbiased and conclusive judgement—are a prejudice in themselves, Gadamer rightly argues; a disabling prejudice in this case. They obscure a key insight into human understanding itself in their failure to comprehend the finiteness of the human mind and the insurmountable fallibility of even the best of humankind's intellectual efforts. Acknowledging and disciplining such excessive claims, Gadamer continues, "opens the way to an appropriate understanding of the finitude which dominates not only our humanity but also our historical consciousness" (Gadamer, 1989, p. 276).

On Gadamer's account, every instance of human understanding proceeds from a background of previous influences, not from an exercise of reason that has been cleansed of all preconceptions. This background predisposing of our efforts to know and understand, Gadamer argues, is just what inescapably "happens to us above our wanting and doing." Furthermore, much of this influential historical background, or "effective history" to use Gadamer's term, might *remain* implicit, even where the best efforts of logic and self-criticism are employed to detect its more inconspicuous movements and effects (Gadamer, 1989, p. 300). Tradition is to be understood, and particularly where education is concerned, as the totality of such prior influences. In the German text of *Truth and Method*, two different words are regularly used, apparently interchangeably, for "tradition': *Tradition* and *Überlieferung*. Both are correctly rendered in English as "tradition," but a close look at the makeup of *Überlieferung* suggests a three-part notion like "over-lying-ness," which highlights the pervasive and enduring nature of tradition. To minimize what might be lost in translation, what "tradition" means, in Gadamer's writings can be rendered as a totality of overlying influences, explicit and implicit, that predispose a person in each and every new encounter. The encounter could be with a text, an institution, the claims others make on oneself, and so on. Where education is concerned, and more particularly teaching, something from such a totality seeks to address the students through the agency of the teacher. Or to put it from the students' side: tradition, in one or other of its formal voices (e.g., mathematics, geography, music), seeks to address and engage them through the agency and interpretations of the teacher. Viewed this way, the encounter can properly be seen as a joint undertaking, as distinct from any mere transmission. It is an active interplay where myriad influences, overt and less conspicuous, are already in play, and where many more come into play, momentarily or for longer. A teacher might be regarded as the person who commences this interplay. But it would be more accurate to say that the teacher *steps into* this interplay. They intervene and lead, with a hope of opening up new imaginative landscapes, of cultivating growing fluency and capability among students to respond to what seeks to address them. Teaching, accordingly, would encourage and support students to uncover fresh aspects of their own emergent identities, including their particular possibilities and limitations, and eventually to discover and negotiate further paths of their own.

TRADITION IN MACINTYRE'S WRITINGS

One of MacIntyre's most distinctive contributions to ethics as a field of study, and to ethics in practical action, is the relationship he illustrates among tradition, practice, and virtue. Aristotle's concern with pursuing ethical goods stands continually in the background of MacIntyre's consideration of practices, and this means, he remarks, that he will be using the word *practice* in a way that might not completely agree with ordinary usage (MacIntyre, 1985, p. 187). On MacIntyre's analysis, a practice is not the same as an activity or action that is repeated over and over. Any practice deserving the name, rather, pursues a purpose (*telos*) for which the practice itself came into existence. Taking his cue from Aristotle, but also from Hegel, MacIntyre argues that a practice is a deliberate and cooperative form of activity that has evolved over time; a form of activity that is socially valued, and that pursues some inherent goods that are recognized and shared by its practitioners. Through such pursuits, he continues, the practitioners not only define the practice and its goods. They also *refine* both, developing, through their committed efforts, new capabilities for themselves, new standards for achieving excellence in the practice, and new possibilities for enhancing and extending the practice. Initial examples he gives of practices include farming, architecture, physics, chemistry, biology, the work of the historian. Clarifying further, he distinguishes practices from skills: "Bricklaying is not a practice; architecture is. Planting turnips is not a practice, farming is" (MacIntyre, p. 187).

A practice, when understood in this expanded Aristotelian sense, highlights its inherent goods—for example, in medicine, the studied promotion of health, the diagnosis and treatment of illness, the advancement of research pertinent to both. It also allows these goods to offer themselves as worthy candidates for the energies of practitioners, including aspirant practitioners. A practice is thus the bearer of a tradition of inherent goods, but also of associated virtues, for example, perseverance, open-mindedness, resilience, willingness to seek criticism, dedication to improvements. In pursuing with integrity the inherent goods of the practice the practitioners become habituated in the associated virtues. But in practicing such virtues they also transcend the particular goods of the practice and achieve something of "the *telos* of a whole human life, conceived as a unity" (MacIntyre, 1985, p. 202). MacIntyre adds that while there may sometimes be competition to excel among practitioners in pursuing inherent goods, the achievement of these goods is nevertheless an achievement "of the whole community who participate in the practice" (MacIntyre, pp. 190–191). Both the goods of the practice and the associated virtues become borne by the tradition of the practice itself, which seeks its renewal and extension through the efforts of successive generations. Failure in this regard, however, including any failures in educating newcomers to the practice and failures by experienced practitioners, can result in lasting damage. The virtues may give way to vices—lethargy, jealousy, greed. Consequently, the tradition may atrophy rather than strengthen.

Gadamer, like MacIntyre, writes insightfully about practice and practical philosophy, especially in later works where he highlights the importance of *phronesis* and solidarity (Gadamer, 1982). He does not, however, make practice a theme of close investigation to the extent that MacIntyre does, and the connections among practice, virtues, and tradition that are prominent in MacIntyre's writings are more implicit in Gadamer's. But in relation to epistemological questions, or how tradition affects human understanding and knowing, there are some strong parallels. The following passage, for instance, from the later pages of *After Virtue*, could almost have been written by Gadamer.

> For all reasoning takes place within the context of some traditional mode of thought, transcending through criticism and invention the limitations of what had hitherto been reasoned in that tradition; this is as true of modern physics as of medieval logic. (MacIntyre, 1985, p. 222)

Like Gadamer, moreover, MacIntyre rejects the idea that there is some standpoint available to critical thought that can rise above the sweep of history and circumstance, and from where final judgments on the matters that have been risen above can be made. Classic epistemology would regard the lack of such a superior vantage point as a deficiency, to be overcome by philosophical efforts, as distinct from an inescapable human limitation that should be acknowledged. It would regard such an acknowledgment as a capitulation to relativism, for in the absence of a criterion that is independent of time or cultural circumstance, how can one evaluate the truth or falsity of any claims put forward? Indeed, this was the basis of much of the criticism of Gadamer's *Truth and Method* after the appearance of the first German edition, including the criticisms that initiated the Habermas-Gadamer debate of the 1970s (Ricoeur, 1981).

MacIntyre's response to the relativist challenge, particularly in *Whose Justice? Which Rationality?*, is to argue that a tradition's strengths can best be judged by the kind of progress the tradition makes from its first beginnings in pure historical contingency (MacIntyre, 1988, p. 354ff). This involves a critical examination of how successfully or poorly the tradition is able to deal with crises. More specifically, it includes: how well the tradition questions its own texts and authorities; how well it brings to light its own inadequacies; how well it reevaluates and formulates anew its core contents in the light of criticisms (MacIntyre, p. 355). On this account the most likely criterion for evaluating the truth claims associated with any given tradition would seem to be *warranted assertibility*, a criterion notably associated with John Dewey (1938). From the standpoint of warranted assertibility, the claims of a particular tradition would not seek to be absolute, or final. They would seek, rather, to provide a robust defense of themselves, while remaining open to criticisms that enable that tradition to revise and strengthen what warrants its claims.

MacIntyre insists, however, that this is not enough. He rightly points out that the "concept of warranted assertibility always has application only at a particular time and place in respect of standards then prevailing," and he adds: "The concept of truth however is timeless." In other words, if some tradition claims "that some thesis is true," then that is a claim "for all possible time" (MacIntyre, 1988, p. 363). Such a standpoint toward the evaluation of a tradition's truth claims sits ill with MacIntyre's own account of tradition, and with how truth claims might withstand the charge of relativism. Indeed, in the closing pages of *Whose Justice? Which Rationality?* MacIntyre's "true for all possible time" claim yields to a contrasting stance. There, MacIntyre concludes that upholders of the book's Aristotelian-Augustinian-Thomistic thesis "have every reason at *least so far* to hold that the rationality of their tradition has been confirmed in its encounters with other traditions" (MacIntyre, p. 403, emphasis added).

SOME CONFLUENT INSIGHTS

Among the conclusions that can be gathered from these reflections on MacIntyre's and Gadamer's investigations, the following three are decisive for understanding the significance of tradition for education. First, MacIntyre's conclusion that "there are no tradition-independent arguments to appeal to" in evaluating truth claims echoes strongly the tenor of argument in Gadamer's *Truth and Method*, and indeed in hermeneutic philosophy more widely. Variants of this conclusion, moreover, are also shared by pragmatist philosophy (Bernstein, 2010), and by prominent analytic philosophers such as John McDowell, Hilary Putnam, and Donald Davidson. It is a conclusion that reminds educational effort that its own best understandings are never more than partial, and in both senses of that word: (a) incomplete, (b) affected by bias. Second—and this point has two aspects—tradition in its fuller ontological sense as totalities of influences becomes education's stock-in-trade. And, linked to this, education is now seen as being particularly responsible for how encounters with tradition are made enabling, fruitful, and as far as possible justifiable. Third, there is a necessity for education—more particularly for teaching—to understand itself *as* a tradition. The distinctive good, or aim, of this tradition isn't that of passing on anything "traditional." Rather, it is that of furnishing and enhancing, from its own resources as a tradition, a family of practices that make encounters with inheritances of learning fruitful, defensible, and self-sustaining. The task of tracing in outline the main features of teaching *as* a tradition lies before us now, and in this case, it will be necessary to review some important differences between Gadamer and MacIntyre.

EXPLORING TEACHING AS A TRADITION

What is distinctive about teaching *as* a tradition is that, as a specific tradition, it differs from what might normally be meant by this term: for example, a Puritan tradition, a civil rights tradition, a behaviorist research tradition, a feminist tradition, and so on. Specific traditions of this kind are keenly conscious of rival traditions. Accordingly, when seeking to renew and extend themselves, opposition to other traditions features more centrally in their efforts than would be the case if other traditions were not seen as rivals. Where teaching as a specific tradition is concerned, it is distinctive in being both deeply committed *and* nonpartisan. Its specific character springs from its responsibility to tradition as a totality of influences, and to making that totality more inclusive in the case of the particular topic or subject being studied. This tradition's orientation and focus *are educational before they are anything else*. Its inherent purpose is to enable pupils and students (of whatever age) to engage with inheritances of learning so that new imaginative neighborhoods are opened up and new inquiries are got underway.

There are two stances in MacIntyre's argument, however, that seem incompatible with the characterization just drawn. The first is his insistence that "genuinely to adopt the standpoint of a tradition thereby commits one to its view of what is true and false, and in so committing one, prohibits one from adopting any rival standpoint" (MacIntyre, 1988, p. 367). The second is his insistence that "teaching itself is not a practice, but a set of skills put to the service of a variety of practices" (MacIntyre & Dunne, 2004, p. 5). These initially look like unwelcome objections to the case for teaching as a tradition in its own right, but exploring their substance may help to clarify important elements of that very case. In relation to the first point—that commitment to a tradition requires opposition to rival standpoints—MacIntyre holds to the stance that tradition must be partisan. Indeed, his criticisms of the liberal university underline this, as does his vision of what the university's educational mission should look like (MacIntyre, 1988, p. 399ff; 1990, p. 216ff). University teachers, in MacIntyre's vision, especially in the humanities, would have a double role. The first would be to advance inquiry from within a particular tradition, while entering into controversy with the conflicting standpoints of other traditions. This would also involve testing and retesting "the central theses advanced from one's own point of view against the strongest possible objections to them to be derived from one's opponents" (MacIntyre, p. 231). The second role would be "to uphold and to order the ongoing conflicts," while seeking to ensure that rival standpoints were not "illegitimately suppressed" (MacIntyre, p. 231). This would sustain each contending standpoint in "advancing its own partisan account of the nature and function of objectivity" . . . in "an arena of conflict in which the most fundamental kind of moral and theological disagreement was accorded recognition" (MacIntyre, p. 231).

Two points here are pertinent for our exploration: first, MacIntyre's emphasis on sustaining an ethos where earnest disagreement is not only tolerated but invited; second, his insistence that rival standpoints are not suppressed. These two points are not only compatible with teaching as a committed and nonpartisan tradition. Both describe an exercise of virtues by university teacher practitioners. They are in fact key features of the kind of interplays that constitute teaching as a practice in its own right. But his demand for partisanship in the university's teaching stance as a whole is coercive. It changes the underlying context and orientation. This demand makes the practices of the university, or college or school, subordinate to a controlling body, whose doctrines and policies set the tenor of the learning to be pursued. The curious exemplar MacIntyre gives in support of his argument is the University of Paris in the 13th century, where the controlling body was the church (MacIntyre, p. 232).

We will return to this issue in a moment, after considering MacIntyre's other contention: that "teaching itself is not a practice, but a set of skills put to the service of a variety of practices." This claim can be granted if "teaching" is understood in a limited sense as a means to an end, or a specific ingredient in a practice—like the skill of planting turnips in relation to the practice of farming. In debating this point with Joseph Dunne (MacIntyre & Dunne, 2004), MacIntyre declares, however, that "teaching is never more than a means. . . . All teaching is for the sake of something else and so teaching does not have its own goods" (MacIntyre & Dunne, p. 8). This stance is strangely at odds with what he says about university teaching upholding particular traditions, as cited in the two previous paragraphs. The inconsistency can, of course, be removed if teaching is considered in the fuller sense of an occupational commitment, as Hansen does throughout his writings. In fact, MacIntyre himself comes back to something like this position just a little later in his exchange with Dunne: "And, as with other practices, achieving the ends of teaching requires that teachers engage in the practice of making and sustaining the communal life of the school" (MacIntyre & Dunne, p. 8). Notwithstanding these apparent inconsistencies, MacIntyre's contrasting stances on teaching may nevertheless help to illustrate the following important point. Where teaching is properly conceived—as a practice as distinct from a set of discrete skills—it offers manifold possibilities to participate in and uphold a tradition. This can be done in a sometimes partisan sense as understood by MacIntyre, or in the more universal sense arising from Gadamer's insights.

To someone who shares the partisan emphasis in MacIntyre's stance, it will probably seem that conceiving of teaching as a tradition in its own right is a less committed or a more neutral kind of engagement. It lacks the wholehearted commitment to tradition in the form of a *telos* embodied in some "ism." But to conclude thus is to overlook some key insights that Gadamer's investigations of the structure of human understanding make available. Again, it is worth recalling Gadamer's insistence that his intention is not to support this or that cause but to honor the "scientific" integrity (*wissenschaftliche Redlichkeit*) involved in philosophical activity itself, and thus to illuminate "what happens to us above our wanting and doing" when understanding (including mis-understanding) takes place (Gadamer, 1989, p. xxviii). Gadamer's researches have highlighted just how inescapably human efforts to understand take place *within* a larger play of influences. A disciplined and self-critical consciousness can be helpful in bringing to light and discriminating between influences that predispose us in ways that open up minds and hearts, or in ways that are imprisoning or distorting. But even the most incisive or circumspect self-consciousness cannot disclose all of these influences and make them available for inspection (Gadamer, p. 542ff). This can be seen as bad news for the classic aspirations of epistemology. More importantly, however, it recalls the original insight in Socrates's declaration in the *Apology* (23a) that "real wisdom is the property of God" and that human wisdom is paltry by comparison. Such insights offer a distinctive orientation for any human undertakings dedicated to the betterment of human knowing, particularly undertakings like teaching.

Elucidating this orientation, the main emphasis of teachers' work is disclosed as that of introducing newcomers, or comparative newcomers, to what one or more of the voices of tradition seek to say to them. Faithfulness to this purpose does not involve the teacher as a partisan representative of any of these voices. Yet the history of education has so many instances of partisan pedagogy that many find it difficult to envisage what teaching as a nonpartisan but committed practice might look like. An example may help to illustrate, and to conclude. Let the voice in question be that of history and the topic being explored be the Reformation. Insofar as the teacher's own engagement with tradition is conversationally alive and fruitful, the teaching-learning experience might be something like this: The teacher initially dramatizes the key issues by offering a robust case for Luther, and then a robust case for the Vatican. More importantly, the teacher now engages the pupils in focused research of the pertinent historical issues. Collectively and individually they explore merits and shortcomings in the cases to be made for both sides, and for the other parties that enter the picture as the historic drama unfolds. A new imaginative landscape is thus opened up for the pupils, and in ways that progressively involve qualities like analysis, tracing of inferences, discernment, and judgment. Whatever the field, or the topic, the teacher's actions are neither those of a partisan nor a transmitter. They are rather those of a pedagogical leader who quickens the interests of the pupils by seeking to accomplish a productive frisson between the horizons of the pupils and the inheritances of learning that seek to address them. No less important is the teacher's vigilant monitoring of the experiences that take place, and not just of the pupils' achievements as recorded by examinations and tests. It also includes careful attention to changes in the pupils' *attitudes toward* what they are studying—for example, motivations, study energies, resilience. It includes further a regular monitoring of their *capable practices of* learning—for example, capacity to research emergent issues, to cooperate with fellow pupils, to question and investigate, to lay out and present their work.

If one is to insist on a *telos* for teaching, as MacIntyre does for anything that counts as a virtuous practice, that *telos* is to be realized—or frustrated—in pedagogical practice itself as it endeavors to step into tradition as play of influences. More concretely, it is to be realized in the integrity of a teacher's daily efforts, as embodied in a family of actions such as those sketched in the previous paragraph, or furnished in abundance in David Hansen's work.

REFERENCES

Bernstein, R. J. (2010). *The pragmatic turn*. Polity Press.

Dewey, J. (1938). *Logic: The theory of inquiry*. Henry Holt & Company.

Gadamer, H.-G. (1982). *Reason in the age of science* (F. G. Lawrence, Trans.). The MIT Press.

Gadamer, H.-G. (1989). *Truth and method* (J. Weinsheimer & D. G. Marshall, Trans.; 2nd rev. ed.). Continuum. (Original work published 1960)

Hansen, D. T. (1995). *The call to teach*. Teachers College Press.

Hansen, D. T. (2001). *Exploring the moral heart of teaching: Toward a teacher's creed*. Teachers College Press.

Hansen, D. T. (2011). *The teacher and the world: A study of cosmopolitanism as education*. Routledge.

MacIntyre, A. (1985). *After virtue: A study in moral theory*. (2nd ed.). Duckworth.

MacIntyre, A. (1988). *Whose virtue? Which rationality?* Duckworth.

MacIntyre, A. (1990). *Three rival versions of moral enquiry*. Duckworth.

MacIntyre, A. & Dunne, J. (2004). Alasdair MacIntyre on education: In dialogue with Joseph Dunne. In J. Dunne & P. Hogan (Eds.), *Education and practice: Upholding the integrity of teaching and learning* (pp. 1–17). Blackwell.

Ricoeur, P. (1981). Hermeneutics and the critique of ideology. In J. B. Thompson (Ed.), *Hermeneutics and the human sciences* (pp. 63–100). Cambridge University Press.

CHAPTER 8

Teaching

A Moral Adventure

Catie Bell

David Hansen demonstrated that teaching is a moral endeavor, and this belief has continued to inspire and give substance to my practice for more than three decades. In the mid-1980s, David was a graduate student in the University of Chicago's Department of Education. I had begun teaching 6th grade at the University's Laboratory School. David was a student of Philip W. Jackson, a Dewey expert and the David Lee Shillinglaw Distinguished Service Professor in Education and Psychology, who taught philosophy. Naturally, David found himself deeply immersed in abstract reasoning. In contrast, I spent my days alive to the visceral, concrete activities of energetic 12- and 13-year-olds, work I enjoyed most when it took place outside of the classroom, in those days of rooms structured by straight rows of desks or rectangular tables. Authentic experiences, or so I believed, inspired students to discover and solve practical problems. Intellectual activity that verged on being too theoretical, distant from sensory experience, and actual predicaments made me wary.

For example, without question, my idea of teaching began with the direct experience. Witnessing a naturalization oath ceremony gives rise to wonder about the meaning of citizenship. Middle schoolers, performing folktales at a Head Start program, mediate story's power to hold children spellbound. The challenge of ascending a vertical rock face provides the climber with metaphors transferable to dealing with frustrations in other venues. Putting the concept before the experience, reversing the pedagogical sequence, invites thoughts that rely on mere custom or fantasy or talking about nothing more than air. With 10 years of teaching under my belt, I enjoyed working with adolescents but not so much in the classroom, an environment that struck me as artificial, confining, and, at times, dispiriting. Theory, thin, dry and artificial, seemed too detached from energetic, curious, mysterious, and physically active 6th-graders. Those were the days when I fancied myself an anti-intellectual.

It was not until I met David that I began to glimpse everyday tasks as potential expressions of being "called to teach." David pointed to deeper layers of significance in every facet of work, in or out of the classroom, everything from the sound of my voice to the room arrangement, especially when I neglected to restore tables and chairs so the present class could enjoy the sense of a fresh start. I found discerning potential for moral meaning in quotidian activities at once thrilling and sobering. I kept stopping to wonder: Does this work toward students' best interests? What qualities am I cultivating? In myself? In my students? Am I being fair, compassionate, trustworthy, or respectful? The potential for moral significance existed in everything I did, not just what my students directly observed, but my actions outside the classroom, even when they were not watching—my life, the daily work of becoming a person worthy to teach. Long-nurtured dualisms resolved without my attention—the opposition between classroom teaching and field-based adventures, identifying activities as either vicarious or direct, and dichotomies splitting theory from practice and conventional pedagogy from "authentic."

Seeing teaching as greater, deeper, and more enduring than a specific situation allows us to step back to see more of what matters. As David reminded me, Socrates conducted dialogues while walking around the agora. Whereas classroom activities—reading, writing, and discussion—are commonly viewed as sedentary; properly conducted, they are not inactive. Getting one's head around a new idea, reading a big book, and finding the right words to formulate an insight, each entails taking a risk, disturbing the settled, prodding us to reconstruct some part of the world anew. Any of these common classroom activities, in its own right, has the possibility of becoming an adventure on a par with technical climbing. David played a crucial role in my learning to see more clearly. Even changes, over time, become so thoroughly woven into daily activities that they soon seem natural, as if they had always been part of me. I might ask myself, for instance, when did I learn that a class, bursting with heartfelt but contrary opinions, needs to stop talking and write quietly, taking time to distill thoughts before returning to discussion? When did I start providing a shy or tongue-tied student a conspicuously long pause, giving them time to find their words and let their classmates hear their ideas? After knowing David, I came to realize that once a class is underway, I can expect most students to be open, alert, insightful, and engaged. General signs of irritability, defensiveness, and anxiety are warnings for me to change something I'm doing. My taking classroom teaching seriously started with meeting David in the "Moral Life of Schools" project.

"THE MORAL LIFE OF SCHOOLS"

The former University of Chicago's Department of Education was housed in the high Gothic ceilings of Judd Hall, stuck between the Laboratory School's middle and lower schools. Professors, clutching briefcases or books, moved quietly in and out of their offices, occasionally poking out their heads to admonish passing children who, happily ignoring the "Quiet through Judd Hall" sign, chatted too loudly—their feet clattering on the tiled floor. Tucked away on the first floor was Judd Commons, a meeting place conducive to quiet conversation. Wood-paneled and carpeted, it provided comfortable leather furniture and solid wood tables. Large windows faced west, allowing the afternoon sun to pour in. A portrait of Charles Hubbard Judd, an educational psychologist and early department chair, hung on the wall. Professors of education, Lab School teachers, staff and people from throughout the university gathered there for coffee, pastries, and sandwiches. New teachers delighted in spotting Benjamin Bloom, whose educational taxonomy had been required reading. English teachers, recognizing Wayne Booth, the celebrated rhetorician, and Shakespeare scholar David Bevington discovered that they both enjoyed talking to teachers. Short of requests for students to quiet down, mingling in Judd Commons, and occasional classroom visits by graduate students, interaction between the Department of Education and the Lab School seemed insignificant.

And then, during fall quarter of 1987, my second year at Lab, I received an official memo from Mary Jane Yurchak, the Lab School's director, inviting me to apply to become part of a research project in the Department of Education called "The Moral Life of Schools." While flattered to be asked, I found the title put me off. The word *moral* seemed not just stuffy but charged with negative associations, summoning images of righteous, rigid, and unyielding educators, poised to condemn those of us with inferior standards. *Morality* had always seemed to me a ready source of guilt. "If only I had . . . I shouldn't have, I could have. . . ." Of course, the hot button issue "whose morals?" hovers closely. Then there's the tidy precept clinching an Aesop fable: "Honesty is the best policy" or "Never cry wolf." Within days of receiving the invitation, however, curiosity about events in Judd Hall overwhelmed misgivings about the word "moral." I applied. Along with becoming a teacher and getting married later in life, this turned out to be one of the best decisions I ever made.

Although "The Moral Life of Schools" came to mean a wide variety of things to its 23 participants, "stuffy" would not be among them. Philip Jackson and two doctoral students, David Hansen and Robert Boostrom, conducted the study with 18 teachers, a group representing a wide range of ages, ethnicities, career stages, subjects, and grade levels. What did we teachers have in common? We were all schoolteachers in the Hyde Park neighborhood, but from very different schools: public, Catholic, and independent. For 2½ years, from January 1988 until June 1990, twice a month, absent school vacations, we met on Wednesday nights in the well-appointed Judd Commons. Together, after "breaking bread," delicious catered food, we gathered in a circle to participate in a two-hour seminar. Our work evolved organically. Wisely, the researchers ignored requests for firmer guidelines. Diverse, sometimes divided, and often not afraid to speak out, we suffered various bumps. At first, we were suspicious of each other. Teachers worried about being taken seriously. Would we end up guinea pigs, used, misunderstood, and maligned? Did teachers from parochial schools have the edge when it came to morality? One was actually a priest with a collar. Would high school teachers, accustomed to talking to older students, be permitted to dominate? The researchers worked skillfully to address initial fears. Experimenting with different formats, we resolved various tensions, for example, letting the group choose topics, and having teachers take turns chairing meetings. Over time, concerns about differences among us lost traction as our shared discovery pulled us together and forward: a growing awareness of the moral implications of everything we do.

My initial worries about a spirit of righteousness soon dissipated. The researchers sidestepped defining the word *moral*, which freed us from much culture-bound dogma. In addition to organizing the bimonthly dinners, the researchers conducted two taped interviews with each teacher and had permission to drop into our classrooms whenever they chose. David not only visited my classes, but he also accompanied classes on field trips and attended some grade-level meetings. In addition to sitting in on many classes both during the time of the project and after, astoundingly, he ended up spending a whole year studiously observing a single 6th-grade class.

At the time, I had no idea what David hoped to find in my classroom, and at first, this bothered me. Were some lessons more moral than others? If so, which ones? Were my students "moral"? Was I? Although the researchers' grasp of the word moral continued to elude me, I came to trust David. I looked forward to seeing him sitting in the back of the room, awaiting the start of class, knees protruding slightly beyond the edge of a seat designed for a shorter person. Eager to hear his thoughts about teaching and my classroom, I looked forward to meeting with him after school. David's attentiveness, courtly manner, and gentle intelligence disarmed me. His clear, resonant, and mellifluous voice still makes attending to him pleasant and elevates whatever he is talking about. Early on, we shared mutual delight noticing the incongruously large size of 6th-grade boys' feet. Like the overly large paws of an awkward puppy, boys' feet promise potential for growth. A keen observer, with insight into the likes and manners of adolescents, David often caught interactions among students that I missed. That year he came to know my students as well as I did; with the benefit of two pairs of eyes, David and I came to know that class very well.

David does not miss much. The quality of his caring attention invites a deeply human response, one that includes truthful soul-searching. He was attuned to aspects of my practice I had yet to discover. Determined to become a good teacher, I appreciated David's genuine curiosity about my work and his patience. He calmly listened while I struggled to find words to think about his questions. Respectful of my learning process, he took in what I meant, even when verbal expression faltered. In the project, the phrase "we teach ourselves" arose as an important discovery, one we all came to share.

At first, I took hold of a concrete meaning of the phrase. We teachers have to learn the subject matter in our courses. Much of this we end up teaching ourselves. For me, learning more about history, literature, and art turned out to be an unexpected joy. The promise of a new unit drew me to the library to immerse myself in the topic of upcoming lessons, developing a 12- or 13-year-old's point of view, anticipating the questions a 6th-grader might ask. Getting paid to learn seemed like a good deal. Fascinated by concepts like hydraulic civilizations, mythic archetypes, and the specifics of Roman sanitation, I could not wait both to share what I was learning and to hear what my students had to say. While I love studying, teaching, not scholarship, has been my medium. Whereas some of us write essays, my mind jumps to lesson plans. What do students fundamentally need to know so that they can continue to learn about this area of inquiry? Witnessing students delve into an interest, bring their own thoughts into the world, and engage in what may become lifelong passions is genuinely awesome.

Of course, "we teach ourselves" has a more potent moral meaning, one that at first evaded me. For someone who barely understood herself, the thought of being a model of humanity for students made me very uneasy. For instance, I knew myself to be messy, clumsy, disorganized, imprecise, and unclear. A full list of all my shortcomings is frightening. A deep insecurity about standing in front of students inspired my adventures in the outdoors, games, creative dramas, performances, and other engrossing activities. They allowed me to disappear into the background. But the phrase "we teach ourselves," as I understood from the "Moral Life of Schools" project, conveys a certain inevitability. If students potentially learn from everything we do, then we cannot escape serving as models for them. The concept of "ourselves" extends to the way teachers handle space, time, props, rules, and procedures and to all manner of verbal and nonverbal expressions. Through all of these "extensions," students come to see us as people. I had never before stopped to realize that all my assumptions, understandings, biases, beliefs, and dispositions were not merely on view, but also serve as habits available as subject matter. As a result of interaction with me, students might "catch" them, even undesirable ones. The process of becoming more intentional by discovering better and deeper purposes is bumpy, raggedy, messy, and long.

David encouraged me by pointing to good habits I had already "caught" through teaching. For example, on a field trip, getting students to pay attention can be crucial. Lapses can result in an emergency room visit or worse. Better still, over the years, David's own powers of attention began to rub off on me. I "caught" some of his good habits. For instance, as my vision of teaching as vocation opened up, intensifying a longing for deeper meaning, I began to listen more carefully, grasping connections I had previously overlooked. Gradually, I, too, would read John Dewey's *Democracy and Education* (1916) and *How We Think* (1910b), which helped me to think about dispositions as manifestations of actual commitments, expressions of what matters to us. Dewey addresses intellectual virtues like open-mindedness, wholeheartedness, patience, and courage, composed of constellations of habits that allow us to conduct our lives more humanely and intelligently. Throughout our lives we can deliberately strengthen these virtues. We can also trust our students to "catch" such habits from us.

A LESSON ON THE IDEA OF INTEREST

Anyone who spends time in Hyde Park ends up at the Medici restaurant on 57th Street at some point. Old-fashioned booths, exposed brick walls, and tables covered with layers of graffiti—names, images, song titles going back decades, drawn with knives, sharpies, and Bic pens. The Med, as insiders call it, is open for breakfast, lunch, and dinner. David liked having tea at 4:00. We usually slid into one of the booths on the east side toward the back when the restaurant was nearly empty. While sitting there with David, I began to really think about classroom teaching. Head brimming with philosophy, he pushed my reasoning, nudging me, for example, to turn hunches into questions and to give myself time to explain what I meant. During the project, David and I began a conversation about teaching and learning that continues to this day, more than three decades later.

Interest, as concept, became one of the first lessons and an idea to which we often returned. David explained differences between the more common educational word *motive* and interest. The word motive has roots in the old French *motivus*, meaning "to move." We think of a motive as a cause to act in a certain way. Significantly, the effect is to move in one direction. Teachers, tasked with motivating students, commonly use grades, treats, points, and other extrinsic rewards to get their students to make an effort. We tell students, for example, if they do X, a chore, they "get to do" Y, but often the reward bears no meaningful relation to the chore.

In contrast, David explained, interest literally means "to be between." An interested individual, initially curious, makes a connection between themselves and something outside of them. In this sense, interest facilitates the interrelationship between themselves and what they seek to bring closer. Interest directs attention, a magnet pulling concerns toward a person, ushering in subject matter and thwarting distractions. The more the student learns, in many cases, the more interested they become. Learning fuels curiosity. In this sense, interest serves as both a cause for learning and an effect in promoting further inquiry or a condition for learning and a desired consequence of the process. The end depends on the beginning.

The teacher's task, as David explained, becomes fueling curiosity already alive in their students' experience and guiding students in their explorations to strengthen interest in subject matter for its own sake even as they develop a more mature, more objective grasp. Eventually, the subject matter becomes part of an individual. We become our selves by building on our interests. Without some inkling of curiosity on the part of the student, however, the teacher has nothing to draw from or on. Moreover, attempts to create interest may miss the vital unifying connection between, and intrinsic to, the student and subject matter. For instance, instead of paying attention to what is actually transpiring, the child may become focused on getting a good grade, a symbol external to the process. Alternatively, the teacher, enthusiastic about a fun activity or fixed on a specific outcome, might overlook in both the student and the subject matter the next potential stage in fulfilling an embryonic interest. The implication is that the child's interest and that of the adult can exist on the same continuum, a guide to thinking about the correspondence between what excites the child and what will advance their understanding. Hearing David talk about this, something inside me clicked. The idea of interest seemed robust, embodied social and transactional qualities I had intuited as being crucial to educational activities but never put together as a valuable guide to organizing instruction.

FAILING TO SEE

A romantic reverie: Imagine a school where learning experiences are unimpeded by a standardized schedule, a school in which students' interests take precedence over bureaucratic dictates. Instead of ending an inquiry with the sound of a bell, the teacher responds to deeper, more authentic rhythms, those arising from students' curiosity. Teachers in such a setting are free to allow an exploration to run its course. I shudder to recall a time when preoccupation with logistics blinded me to students' interest.

Prior to working at Lab, as a newly minted 7th-grade teacher in a large junior high school, I worried about mechanical units, such as the slots in the school schedule, covering the topics making up my course, fitting the information outlined in the curriculum guide into class periods, and coordinating with colleagues. For example, each unit featured a recommended number of weeks. Curriculum writers regularly assure teachers that time frames are only suggestions. Yet, as a beginner, how does one estimate the length of a single activity, much less the time needed for a whole unit? Inexperience provided a reason to stay close to recommended guidelines, a schedule I could justify. Those of us teaching the same course shared resources—books, library time, films, and guest speakers—all of which had to be put on a calendar. The special education teachers also called for lessons well in advance. Given the complexities of coordinating the allocation of materials and resources, tentative dates soon hardened into rigid deadlines.

Chronically underestimating time frames, I assigned too few days to complete a unit. Moreover, I often lacked a clear sense of purpose, a way to determine the essential and what could be left out; how to think about beginnings, middles, and ends. Those were also the days when I wanted students to like me. When we slowed down, they rolled their eyes, complaining, "But we're so far behind everyone else!" Today, this worry would prompt discussion about what it means to learn. Back then, however, the students' displeasure stung. Feeling bad, I struggled to keep up with other teachers, compressing all the required instruction into the prescribed six or eight-week units. Unwittingly, as I painfully discovered, sticking to the program meant that students had to confine their curiosity to a predetermined time frame. Based on the plans I had learned to make in order to cover the material, every minute of class time counted. Apparently, this did not include an adequate niche for unscheduled bursts of interest.

I am chagrined to remember Tom, who, several weeks after the end of a unit on Native Americans, came to class eager to share three photographs from his grandparents' visit to Cahokia Mounds, the site of a once thriving pre-Columbian city near St. Louis. Weeks earlier, this had been the focus of our study of Mississippian culture (circa 800 CE until 1400). Tom handed me a photograph with a clear image of the gigantic Monks Mound. Spanning 14 acres and reaching 100 feet high, it is the largest earthen monument in the Americas. Tom's grandparents, having trudged up the steep slope to the top, took a picture overlooking two smaller mounds and the Mississippi River. I also recognized the image of what has come to be known as Woodhenge, a ring of long, wooden poles, set in ancient postholes, re-creating what had been an ancient celestial calendar. Looking at Tom's pictures, my unspoken reaction was panic—"Cahokia—that was four weeks ago. We already covered that!" Instead of welcoming Tom's grandparents' snapshots as valuable contributions to our understanding of American history, I gave into a feeling of resentment: publicly, I thanked him; privately, I was vexed.

In retrospect, I should have invited the whole class to celebrate Tom's expression of ongoing interest, but then, looking back, I worried about stealing what I thought to be precious time from the current unit, the American Revolution. After all, what if Tom's photographs prompted students to ask new questions about Cahokia and the mysteries of mound building? Returning to the topic of Cahokia would slow us down. It had become clear that students' interest in death and dying could devour weeks of classes. Privileging the mechanical units of the school calendar, reluctantly, but deliberately, I relegated Tom's treasures to a corner of the bulletin board with a small three-by-five index card explaining: "These photographs were taken by Tom's grandparents during their trip to Cahokia Mounds."

Tom, who had expressed a keen interest in social studies from the start of the year, stopped raising his hand. In addition, his assignments, when he bothered to hand them in, were no longer carefully detailed. Only by trying to make sense of his change did I begin to consider the depth of his disappointment and my own negligence. Tom had been looking forward to the opportunity to share his grandparents' experience with his classmates, to discuss the photographs, to relate some of his grandfather's stories, and to be able to answer his peers' questions. Instead, I had pushed aside his personal interest in Mississippian culture. In addition to his feeling of loss, I sensed his puzzlement with my conduct. How could Tom and his classmates begin to comprehend his teacher's comparative disregard for a subject, which had until only recently been the all-consuming focus of her life? This incident revealed teacherly ignorance on many counts, some, no doubt, I have yet to discover. In addition to my own inauthenticity, including failure to honor students' interest and my own, how could I have overlooked the crucial role family plays in our lives? The wise teacher seeks out family stories. Moreover, the topic of death always deserves time. Like love, friendship, family, art, religion, and war, death is an inexhaustible subject for both students and their teachers. At that time, I lacked a clear idea of my teacher self, much less any understanding of the crucial role a teacher herself plays as a person from whom children learn to be human. For me, learning to attend to expressions of interest, not just students' but my own, provided a path to becoming better.

WHOLEHEARTEDNESS AND THE WAR OF 1812 PHENOMENON

"The War of 1812 Phenomenon" is what I ended up naming an approach to conserving interest in subject matter, something that became increasingly important to me, a classroom version of the sense of privacy I felt sitting in a booth with David at the Med. The idea is that whatever else might be going on in our lives, the students' and mine, and in the lives of our family members, friends, and colleagues, the day I teach the War of 1812 or any other topic, that subject is more important than anything else. This particular idea helps me to produce the quality of single-minded effort that may stand up to the many forces that fragment educational experience. For the most part, nothing else matters during class time but the lesson. Once class begins, I discourage students from leaving or entering the room. Even slipping out to go to the bathroom can interrupt the sustained focus needed to spark interest and conduct inquiry. This attitude also helps me to resist the temptation to be drawn into local dramas, a discussion of a student's alleged suspension, for example, or a particularly ridiculous feature of the dress code. This idea also cautions me when the focus strays too far, what had once been a promising digression has lost its power to enrich the assigned topic, a signal to return to the plan. Like suspending disbelief once the theater curtain opens, when the door closes, the classroom exists in a different time zone.

Because there are days when securing students' attention, much less holding it, seems impossible, this concept, however ironically titled, reminds me that what we are learning is important. The War of 1812, except for the occasional American history buff, at least so far, has not been a big draw. This is not to say that students cannot be pulled in by wondering about certain details: how Britain ended up with Canada, the origin of the song "The Star-Spangled Banner," or the plight of a teenage boy snatched from the street and forced to sail for the British navy. In general, however, individuals do not come to class already eager to learn about this little war. Long before arriving at this event, I count on students having developed habits that allow them to use class time wisely. Among these is relying on their emerging dispositions to respond actively and respectfully in discussion, including trusting them to "really listen" and deliberate before replying. As David pointed out, a class has the power to forge people.

Dewey's vision of schools as democratic communities also inspired me to craft a classroom community in which students felt free to participate fully and authentically. Speaking wholeheartedly from their deepest selves, I hoped they would also see our work as a collective endeavor, trying to understand what it means to be human and especially to conduct ourselves as good people. A surprising number of Lab's students come to school prepared to do just this. Even so, in the classroom, they benefit when the teacher consciously provides opportunities for them to see for themselves the significant difference their own participation makes, a residue of David's taking me seriously. As a classroom teacher, this can be as simple as reading aloud a significant line from an individual's homework, inviting students to present information their classmates will find especially interesting, taking time to connect a divergent thinker's ostensibly wild theory to the topic under discussion, or naming a student's idea after him, such as "Patel's proposition," "Flores's conjecture," or "Miller's axiom." Like me, students who initially resist being forthcoming often benefit from additional encouragement. The comfort of a smaller group may entice a shy student to speak up. There is no substitute, however, for patient listening in a one-on-one setting, a chance for a student to practice talking about subject matter, uninterrupted, with their teacher, someone eager to hear what they have to say—another gift from David.

WHAT BELONGS IN THE CLASSROOM?

Lab's middle school teachers combined history and English into a 7th- and 8th-grade humanities sequence, which lets each teacher spend more time with fewer students. I was proud of my 8th-grade classes, where interest in subject matter prevailed. Rarely, if ever, did students mention grades. When students voiced worries, they concerned finding ways for everyone to have their ideas taken seriously. In their eagerness to solve problems, to make the class better, these students took risks. They were no longer hiding, as many 8th-graders can, behind an attitude of nonchalance. Instead, they clearly made their needs known, especially to determine fair procedures, how much time to allot activities, the composition of groups, or who went first (even if such decisions were left to chance: a dice roll or a card shuffle).

For the culmination of an immigration unit, students told family stories. More oriented toward community building and art expression than academic rigor, students connected the American history they had been studying to their family's experience. Interest in this work was intense. The students clearly loved learning about themselves and each other through researching, writing, performing, and listening to stories. It was Greta's turn. A serious young lady with a thick blond braid, she told a story about her great-grandfather, who, between the world wars, had been a teacher and cartoonist in Nazi Germany. Not only alarmed by what he witnessed in his country, her grandfather felt an obligation to communicate what he saw. His persistence in publicizing his opinions, despite several warnings from the government, put both himself and his family at risk. At first, he was blacklisted. Eventually, the Nazis put him in a concentration camp. Emerging with a keen awareness of the danger he put his family in, he joined the army.

As it turned out, the war was finally ending. When the Allies won, they sent Greta's great-grandfather to a prisoner-of-war camp, where he spent more than a year. Greta concluded her story by pointing out the importance of freedom of expression and the ease with which her own generation took it for granted. She also intimated that in not taking our liberties more seriously, we might have to pay for our negligence one day. Greta looked happy that her story was well received, and called on Ellen, who raised her hand.

"I wanted to hear about what happened to your great-grandfather in the concentration camp," Ellen suggested.

Greta paused for a moment and then said simply, "I thought about including that part of the story, but I didn't feel right about using my great-grandfather's experience for a grade."

A stunned silence fell on the room as students tried to grasp Greta's position. She had expressed a surprising viewpoint. Even as 8th-graders, the class understood the importance of grades. That success in school smoothed the way to success elsewhere was a common conviction. According to the prevailing belief, grades and high test scores became tickets to a top-notch college. Students tried to assure me that attending a first-rate school positions an individual to meet the right people, get an excellent job, and thereby enjoy the security attendant to receiving a large paycheck. A substantial salary, in their view, like good grades, provides visible evidence of well-being.

For some, Greta's reason to leave out a sensational part of her story proved a revelation. Many students had probably never considered if anything in their own lives might be more important than grades. In fact, several, in their opportunism, had become adept at exploiting any resource to improve their standing. Thus, Greta's statement "but I didn't feel right about using my great-grandfather's experience for a grade" contradicted the prevailing formula for achieving the good life. Even so, I sensed that no one wanted to challenge her. They understood that Greta had presented a position they were unprepared to question.

A savvy young lady, Greta must have been aware that her classmates would have preferred a more sensational version of her story. Many students' stories, revealing sensitive aspects of their lives—divorces, alcoholism, drug addiction, and mental illness—suggested that holding back intimate details was not normative. So much so that the class had instituted a confidentiality agreement. Students understood that they were not to take certain stories out of the classroom, into the halls, and into their homes. Accustomed to thinking of that class as a particularly tight community, Greta's refusal to tell a part of her story bothered me.

At that time, I was relieved to see that I had not succumbed to pressure to stay on schedule, as I am wont to do, letting Greta hear only a modicum of feedback while pressing right ahead to the next student's story. Instead, I allowed the class to talk about grades, about their discomfort with them. The more I thought about this episode, however, the clearer it became that Greta's regret was not the result of a misfit between grading and education. She might have just as easily said, "I didn't feel right about using my great-grandfather's experience to become more popular or to satisfy my classmates' fascination with suffering." To Greta, exploiting her great-grandfather's misfortune for gain, in any form, was wrong. Even more than wanting good grades and being popular, as Greta did, she believed that some things do not belong in school. She was not about to taint a part of her family story by using it as part of a class assignment.

Greta's response did not betray any doubt, hint at a moral dilemma, offer a hypothesis to test or even a question to prompt a class discussion, inviting the group to think with her. Had she herself undergone a more involved thinking process, I suspect she would have been moved to give a fuller explanation, one that addressed her decisionmaking, including a process of weighing alternatives. Instead, Greta was resolute. She honored a clear distinction between family and school. What worried me? Her clear distinction undermined my own commitment to authenticity, unifying the subjective and objective, the War of 1812 phenomenon, and my understanding of Dewey, who argues that holding an interest sacred makes it unavailable to examination. I wanted to believe that in sharing family stories, students gained a deeper sense of belonging to the classroom, one that made them eager to participate freely and fully, including asking hard questions.

I wanted to think that there were no forbidden topics, especially not ones arising from a clear line delineating family and classroom.

I remember David telling me the story of a beginning teacher who wept in his office, grieving her failure to construct a democratic classroom. I wince recalling my then sense of certainty, veering on smugness, as I listened to the story, positive that I would never be so literal. Yet there I was, holding to a reading of Dewey that assured me that insofar as human behavior arises from nature, we as a class should be able to submit Greta's decision to the equivalent of a scientific investigation. I imagined that in addition to exploring her reasoning more deeply, we could look at the stories we too would not choose to bring to school and even examine our decisions.

That day, Greta manifested an enviable wholeness, a display of personal belief that transcended my own limited Deweyan perspective. She took the high road, abiding by moral values that had nothing to do with classroom norms and procedures. Despite having to contradict established mores, Greta held to her own principles. Her choice proved so powerful that in a community primed to question, no one dared interrogate her, not even me. I was left to realize that while I, a student of Dewey, wanted to know more about the line my students drew between home and school, this was my interest, not theirs. One of the many questions that become dormant, ready to be awakened at another moment.

These moments keep me returning to the classroom. Had I not participated in the "Moral Life of Schools" project and met David Hansen, I would not have known that everything has the potential to carry moral content—a badly copied worksheet, the decision the teacher makes to back off, and taking time to reflect on educational moments. It was David who made me realize that I have been called to this most ancient and honorable vocation, and I am grateful for this opportunity to keep discovering what matters.

REFERENCES

Dewey, J. (1910a). Science as subject-matter and as method. *Science*, *31*(787), 121–127.

Dewey, J. (1910b). *How we think*. D.C. Heath & Co. Publishers.

Dewey, J. (1916). *Democracy and education*. Macmillan Company.

CHAPTER 9

Philosophy of the Voice in *The Call to Teach*

Anna Pagès

FOREWORD TO A READING

I first read David Hansen's *The Call to Teach* (1995) in Spanish translation[1] when doing my PhD research on hermeneutics as a philosophy of education. The touchstone of my research was Hans-Georg Gadamer's *Truth and Method* (1989). I was inspired by Gadamer's concept of *understanding*, and took it as a central notion and guidepost in the search for polysemic meaning in different educational settings. At that time, reading *The Call to Teach* became a lesson in the use of understanding as a basis for a historical and personal approach to the world, as a way of looking at values and especially at teachers' lives. Hansen's approach to educational practice made space for a wide variety of small stories, biographies, and cultural experiences. The concepts of plurality, polysemy, and (especially) polyphony were all thrown into sharp relief as I became progressively aware of key problems in education and how philosophy of education might shed light on them.

Gadamer uses the notion of *prejudice* to highlight how we arrive in the world with a vision of the good and the beautiful, a vision we inherit from past generations and that molds our present. In this sense, tradition constitutes a framework of meaning, where education acts as a living conversation between the experience of the past and the expectations for the future:

> In understanding tradition not only are texts understood, but insights are acquired and truths known. But what kind of knowledge and what kind of truth? (Gadamer, 1989, p. xxi)

The term *voice* is foundational in the search for a different kind of truth. For Gadamer, it occupies a principal role where "insights are acquired" throughout an ongoing historical conversation (Gadamer, 1989, p. xxi). It refers to, on the one hand, the limitation and fallibility of time and, on the other, to history, the latter being defined as the impact of the past on the present. The term also suggests a view of tradition as an unfathomable experience (Pagès, 2006). These are the cornerstones of a truly humanistic education.

In revisiting *The Call to Teach*, I focus on the notion of voice as being key to the act of understanding. The concept of voice is one that goes beyond the notion of *logos*, reflected in Aristotle's discussion of the relationship between *logos* and voice in his *On Interpretation* (1963), a text that has awakened the interest of a number of philosophers, including Aubenque (1962), Whitaker (1996), and Agamben (2017). Recent contributions by feminist philosophers, such as the Italian Adriana Cavarero (2005), have shed light on the issue of the voice and vocal expression as a way of asserting the existence and importance of marginal traditions, as voices that have been excluded from the philosophical canon.

In this chapter, I will argue for the possibility of reading *The Call to Teach* from the notion of voice, not only as a literary metaphor, but as a problem to be addressed from within the text itself. *The Call to Teach* can be read as a philosophy of the voice. It serves as an example of how the notion of voice is brought to life inside real teaching practice, as a token for innovative, noninterchangeable, and concrete educational experience. This particular approach to the voice as a form of expression also allows us to discuss how contemporary education can foster more fruitful relations between theory and practice in the service of encouraging "an individual sense of agency" (Hansen, 1995, p. 10).

THE VOICE IN THE LANGUAGE OF VOCATION

In his work, Hansen underscores the importance of the language of vocation as a means of describing and explaining teaching. The term *vocation* evokes both public service and personal fulfillment, suggesting an exterior and interior movement, a voice from without and one from within. Neither can exist without action or embodiment: "Vocation cannot exist as a state of mind alone, disembodied or removed from a practice" (1995, p. 5). Both movements are described throughout the text, in order to convey that the practice of teaching takes the shape of an original expressive action, and a building up of closer relation with others.

Hansen strives to provide an answer to the question "Who, or what, is [a] calling?" We can clearly identify at least three sources, or "calls" within the text:

a. the voice of the four teachers whom Hansen studies, and their respective stories;
b. the voice of the students, which Hansen reports with extreme subtlety in his descriptions of the class atmosphere and the various conflicts taking place there; and

    c. the voice of the author himself, interpreting the other voices
       through a philosophical orientation to education.

Is it possible to read without the eyes? Not quite. But, in fact, *The Call to Teach* does give us the impression that as we read, we are also listening to these intermingling voices. We read with a special listening activity. Hansen teaches us to be good listeners to the ongoing experience of education, showing that philosophy of education is an endeavor of listening to real and engaging everyday educational encounters.

Adriana Cavarero (2005) begins her reflection on the voice with reference to the Italian writer Italo Calvino and his short story "A King Listens," which describes a realm where political control is exerted strictly by listening: the king sits on his throne and listens to all the sounds he can hear from the kingdom. One day, a woman's voice is heard singing outside a window in the darkness. The tonality and the sound of that voice, coming from inside a living person, introduces a division between "cold" sounds without meaning on the one hand, and the unique and singular warming presence of a person's voice on the other. For Cavarero, the vitality of the voice upends the politics of a fictional kingdom and introduces a sense of uniqueness to individual expression. Working from everyday teaching experience, Hansen articulates a vision of the human voice, not only as a bit of empirical evidence, but as a sound coming from a living "vibration of a throat of flesh" (2005, p. 2). In this way, the voice is a real reference for the representation of teaching. Similarly, Hansen states that vocation is by its very nature a noninterchangeable, personalized notion, one that only takes on its full meaning for teachers in their respective classrooms: "[Their] language is that of vocation—an idiom that takes us *into*, not away from, their experience as individuals" (1995, p. 147).

Teaching is not simply a function to be subjected to accountability controls. Instead, it is a form of imagination and an expression of interest, in the Deweyan sense, where the idea of *interest* represents something more than mere preference. The voice becomes a source of interest, beyond the *logos* as a detached stance toward an object:

> The interest one shows in some larger concern or issue helps to shape the person's beliefs, convictions, and attitudes. Interest draws out the person's mind and imagination. It fuels greater curiosity, fascination, and even wonder. It implies not a detached stance toward the object but an involved one, such that one's interest influences how one sees that object and orients oneself to it. (1995, p. 144)

The notion of the voice beyond philosophical *logos* is explored by Giorgio Agamben in his article "Experimentum Vocis" (2017),[2] where he offers a reading of Aristotle's *On Interpretation*. Agamben theorizes the idea of a voice that can revive philosophy, breathing new life into it. His thesis is that a certain voice might serve as a nexus between the living being and the written word, a place for a historical encounter between tradition, on one side, and spoken language (and real life) on the other. In this sense, personal understanding might articulate both the dimension of semantics and semiotics through the intimate experience of a talking voice. In this work, Agamben suggests that contemporary philosophy must adopt a new approach in order to recover the lost voice in the language of philosophy. Ultimately, what Agamben is attempting is to highlight the importance of the *logos* incarnated in the existential voice, moving away from the universal and toward greater individual uniqueness, so as to recover ignored and marginalized voices.

In *The Call to Teach*, we can grasp a number of these small voices, those of educators who go unrepresented according to the prevailing view of teaching as a profession. Hansen brings these voices to life by recounting the nuances of everyday experience, spotlighting the everyday difficulties, worries, and problems faced by the teachers he depicts (Ms. Payton, Mr. Peters, Mr. James, and Ms. Smith). With the stories of these four teachers, the book enshrines heretofore missing or unheard speaking voices, recording them as they try to understand what is happening in their classrooms and to determine the best course of action in various circumstances. For Agamben, the philosophical search for truth is not enough. Any reflective endeavor must also include the passion of a voice (such as the voice of teaching) without which any account of the human experience is inevitably incomplete. Philosophy can thus be defined as the search for a voice.

In his analysis of Aristotle's *On Interpretation*, C. W. A. Whitaker details Aristotle's account of the voice text as follows:

> We are first told that spoken utterances are "symbols" of affections in the soul, and that writing likewise consists of symbols of spoken utterances. He then goes on to say that, just as written letters are not the same for everyone, neither is speech; the affections in the soul, however, for which speech stands, are the same for everyone, as are the things of which the affections in the soul are likenesses. The same spoken sound, then, can be represented in different written marks: the nature of the sound does not determine how this must be done. In the same way, the same affections in the soul may be represented by different utterances; there is a variety of languages spoken, just as there is a variety of systems of writing in use. (Whitaker, 1996, pp. 145–147)

It is helpful to highlight a particular feature of Whitaker's observation on the spoken: the fact that there is no exact correspondence among sound, speech, and written marks: "[The] nature of the sound does not determine how this must be done" (Whitaker, 1996, p. 145).

In other words, although we may try to transcribe what the voice is tell-ing us, there is no command or general rule to follow. This writing can be done in a multiplicity of manners, depending on the language and the con-text. In a certain way, this is also what *The Call to Teach* shows us: that we can represent the voice from a wide range of places, stories, conflicts, and situations, none of which in and of themselves is able to paint a total or fully accurate picture of reality. Every teacher's voice emerges from a complex, ambiguous, unfathomable act of representation.

Whitaker goes on to explain the origin of the word *symbol* as *token* in ancient Greece:

> What is important is that the choice of a token, unlike a tool, is not determined by the task for which it is chosen. Any sound may be chosen to denote any ob-ject. There is, indeed, the requirement that the word should be audible, but, as we shall see, a sound is meaningful by virtue of being adopted as a token, not because it can be heard. (Whitaker, 1996, p. 145)

In short, the function of words can be compared to that of a token, rather than that of a tool. The choice of one sound or another is nothing more than an arbitrary convention. Elsewhere, in the section on "Human Speech and Inarticulated Utterances," Whitaker (1996, pp. 47–50) points out that according to Aristotle there are two defining characteristics of the voice: first, the voice is made by a living thing, requiring the lungs and wind-pipe; second, the voice accompanies some imagination, which is why the soul is responsible for a voice. The idea that the voice is said to be meaning-ful gives us the notion that when we identify a voice, we are thus in the realm of meaning. But a voice by itself constitutes an open meaning. It needs to be understood by a reader or a listener who is thus able to identify a range of meanings.

Reading *The Call to Teach*, the language of vocation can be compared to a kind of philosophy of the voice, standing in contrast to the universal *logos* of philosophy, understood as a discourse that seeks Truth and Beauty in the Platonic sense. Hansen opens up a voice as something to be partially signified. Through his ethnographic study of the four school settings and teachers, Hansen shows different kinds of tokens, coming together to build a polysemy, and sketching the contours of the concept of a calling (and of being called) as manifest in teaching experience. Here we have an interest-ing conception of what philosophy can be: a struggle to seek out incarnated voices (i.e., tokens to be signified), moving beyond a closed discourse of well-established and standard meanings. The language of vocation is pitted against the language of profession.

Following this approach, we can now analyze three different kinds of voices that feature in *The Call to Teach*. This will help us identify the expressive forms of the voice in the text as well as determine them from a philosophical perspective. All three represent ways to deploy voice or vocation in teaching:

a. voice as subjectivity (tone)
b. voice as fallibility (moral conscience)
c. voice over time (resonance)

VOICE AS SUBJECTIVITY (TONE)

Tone of voice appears as one of the central features of everyday practice in the four teachers' classrooms. These teachers adapt the intensity of their tone to suit educational purposes. In the text, one witnesses how tone of voice reflects teacher subjectivity: It can express anguish, impatience, fragility in the face of conflict, or a desire to help struggling students. Subjectivity is reflected in tone of voice as it evolves with classroom events and circumstances. By bringing tone of voice to the foreground, Hansen also represents a major element of a teacher's agency.

Ms. Payton, a science teacher, has a strong tone of voice. Hansen entitles one of the sections on this teacher as "The Look and Sound of Engagement," often emphasizing with capital letters her loud voice for readers to hear. Ms. Payton is keenly aware that her voice serves as a useful tool in her teaching activities:

> She explains that she deliberately uses her voice to obtain students' attention and cooperation. She does so, in part, to compensate for what she regards as her short physical stature. (Hansen, 1995, p. 26)

It is not clear, though, whether Ms. Payton shares this interpretation of the voice as a way to compensate for her lack of height. She knows that having a "big voice" can be relevant in the everyday struggle of teaching:

> I've never really felt that the students gave me a hard time because of my stature. They generally can see past that, especially when they hear my big voice that just resounds in the room, and they don't know what to do about it. . . . When I get really loud with students, it's a shock to them—That is not done here! (Hansen, 1995, p. 26)

Ms. Payton explains the difference between 7th-graders and high school students, saying that the former "will pick up on the tone of your voice and get really upset about it" (Hansen, p. 28). For her, tone of voice is a teaching tool, as much as a learning activity. At the same time, the representation of her voice gives the reader an idea of who she is. Ms. Payton exudes self-confidence in her ability to manage the class and regularly reassures students regarding the agenda of activities: "She wants her students to understand unambiguously how to conduct themselves so that they can concentrate on their academic work" (Hansen, p. 28).

Mr. Peters, the religion teacher, is very sensitive to noise: "Lift your chairs when you move them! Remember the library is just below us!" (Hansen, 1995, p. 49). His sensitivity corresponds with his rising and falling tone of voice. Hansen describes this small but beautiful detail by highlighting certain expressions:

> "Okay, let's stop," said Mr. Peters, hand on chin and looking at the floor. The class was silent. After a moment, he averred: "Actually, you can do scientific studies to prove that we are descended from apes. But look," his voice suddenly rising, "what about your future?" . . . "Okay," said Mr. Peters in a tone that announced the close of discussion. (Hansen, 1995, pp. 49–51)

Hansen repeatedly refers to Mr. Peters's tone of voice to make the reader aware of this teacher's sensitivity to students' difficult situations and the wish to serve their educational needs as best he can. Mr. Peters is often observed exhorting the students to develop their own opinions, without ever shouting or imposing his perspective on others: "I've never been one to go out and shout, you know, Jesus Christ is Lord," (Hansen, 1995, p. 62) he explains. He wants the children to identify their own beliefs, and so the most important rule for Mr. Peters is not to push them: "I don't want them to have anything stuffed down their throats" (Hansen, p. 62). Hansen adds: "He engaged students in systematic reading aloud in class of the Bible, particularly the Gospels, accompanied by discussion of the text's meanings" (Hansen, p. 46).

The respect that Mr. Peters shows his students has to do with letting them think for themselves, while at the same time providing them with the personal space they need to do so: "The incessant religious talk these students have heard has ended up producing a resentment against it" (Hansen, 1995, p. 59). Mr. Peters is also attuned to the slightest expression of struggle in his students and aware of the importance of listening to each other: "Make sure we're listening, c'mon guys!" (Hansen, p. 47).

Mr. James, the special education teacher, is determined never to raise his voice to his students: "He rarely raises his voice, even when he is confronting students for bullying their mates or teachers, for not doing their work, for taking advantage of him" (Hansen, 1995, p. 68). In Mr. Peters's case, the strong voice that comes from outside the class is the "collective cry from his colleagues—'get them out of my classroom!'" (Hansen, p. 69). The other teachers often voice their incredulity, expressing disbelief in the progress of Mr. James's students. He is constantly being "called on to adjudicate disputes and resolve disagreements concerning students in the program"

(Hansen, p. 71). He chooses not to shout at students: "I used to shout at them—but that just didn't work. They are used to shouting and being shouted at everywhere they go" (Hansen, p. 77). This is corroborated by Hansen, who, in his turn, says, "He does not fight verbally with students or shout at them, or intimidate or humiliate them" (Hansen, p. 77).

We are in the presence of a protective person, a teacher who works to ease students' path and perhaps remove some of the obstacles that those in his special education class face. He defines himself as a kind of shepherd or a "plague fighter," trying to remain "tuned into the students": "With special students, showing that you are tuned into them and listening to their problems is number one" (Hansen, 1995, p. 77). He is committed to listening to these voices from the margins the students represent. His quiet tone is by no means a weak one, but rather the expression of strong purpose. Here, Hansen references the work of Kounin (1968), who describes experienced teachers as having the quality of "withitness" (Hansen, 1995, p. 111).

Ms. Smith recognizes subtle changes in the classroom by identifying the changes in her voice. In fact, she describes this as a split in her subjectivity, manifest in the voice, when she says:

> There is a voice that doesn't sound like my voice, that will come in when I'm strained and I'm not being honest any more. I'm not comfortable in the situation. I'm fighting back, I'm fighting with myself. And all of a sudden I'll hear that tone, and I know that I've got to change the activity, that I'm out of sync. (Hansen, 1995, p. 111)

She hears her voice as though it issues from outside her, suggesting she is capable of listening to herself. She can hear her own voice, not only in the sense of her internal consciousness, but also as an entity that is something other-than-herself. The voice of the teacher can be heard by the very person engaged in the teaching act, capable of listening to herself both inside and outside the classroom. It follows that teaching consists in using the voice, rather than simply applying instructional tools or methods.

The tone of voice of each of the four teachers in the text reflects both distinct individuality and split subjectivity. In other words, teachers observe themselves as if from the outside in order to arrive at insights into their own practice through the fluctuations of the voice. Tone of voice can help call a teacher's attention to small details in the practice—in fact, it is one of those details. Tone of voice acts like a ship's compass, guiding students toward new questions and assisting teachers in revisiting meanings long taken for granted. Tone of voice thus becomes a metaphor for a real experience taking place, as Calvino, quoted by Cavarero, would put it, "in a throat of flesh" (2005, p. 2).

VOICE AS FALLIBILITY (MORAL CONSCIENCE)

The four teachers in *The Call to Teach* all try to give rationales for their unique teaching practices, what Hansen defines as a "distinctive personal stamp." Hansen conveys the evolving conflicts, the haunting questions, and the difficult deliberations each teacher confronts over the course of 2 years. These four teachers all possess an acute sense of the moral, expressed in their own inner voices. Hansen gives the moral a special emphasis in the book. He underlines the importance of the language of vocation as a "persistent whisper that seems to say: Try teaching" (Hansen, 1995, p. 125). In addition to being an intellectual endeavor, teaching is always a moral one as well. Moral judgment emerges as a voice coming from inside us. Whenever teachers offer their ideas, recommendations, and guidance, they expose "their moral and educational standards" (Hansen, p. 122).

The moral conscience, as an inner voice that gets formulated in a variety of educational dispositions and situations, is never a complete or absolute feature. This becomes a crucial distinction between Hansen's work and a more Derridean metaphysical perspective on the voice as a presence (Cavarero, 2005). As Cavarero puts it:

> [The] voice is not investigated because of its pertinence to a culture or an age that is opposed to metaphysics, which gets understood as the historical product of a civilization of writing. Rather, the voice is identified by Derrida as the constitutive feature of metaphysics itself, while the task of destabilizing the phonocentric order of metaphysics is reserved for writing. (Cavarero, 2005, p. 214)

In *The Call to Teach,* we find a radically different approach, which Cavarero would surely find to be successful in avoiding the pitfalls of Derridean phonocentrism. There is a voice in the writing of the text, but it is situated within a complex, ambiguous daily practice, rather than within the realm of the metaphysical. In other words, Hansen develops his language of vocation from an anti-Derridean perspective. Here the voice is not viewed as a presence (metaphysics), but as a locus of action, from where a voice can be heard. This is, in *The Call to Teach,* a moral voice standing for the good, emerging from within the practice of teaching.

The notion of a moral voice in teaching becomes credible because it gives the reader a sense of belonging to the common and difficult task of teaching at school. When Hansen refers to the moral voice of teachers, he is not issuing a universal command to be followed in every case. On the contrary, he highlights the fact that teaching is a complicated practice, insisting on the fallible dimension of teaching. The teacher must face everyday choices without ever being certain of the right answer. If there are guidelines that inform teaching, they arise from specific circumstances, undergoing a process of constant change and transformation. From Hansen's precise and delicate transcription of actual teaching practice, the moral voices of these four teachers reverberate throughout the text.

In his Seminar X *On Anxiety*, from 1962–1963, Jacques Lacan (2004) defines the voice as a lost object, referring to it as a sound coming from the exterior. Lacan gives the example of the sound of the *shofar* in the Jewish tradition: the sound of a horn as metaphor for the voice of consciousness emanating from afar, through the commandment "remember." It is then possible to understand the voice as something to be reappropriated by someone, in a movement of incorporation. Teaching can be described as this kind of movement, its content being the different dimensions of practice and cultural memory in school. On the other hand, in *The Call to Teach*, we witness the isolation of the object-voice from a perspective far removed from the philosophical canon. Hansen draws a line through the teachers' four stories by asking a basic question: How did these teachers happen to all go about developing their own tentative, fragile, and nonnormative moral judgment?

In his *Nichomachean Ethics* (2009), Aristotle emphasizes the notion of *phrónesis*—good sense—as a kind of action that reveals who we really are, as a mirror of ourselves and what we stand for. In Hansen's terms: "Vocation implies looking in the mirror" (1995, p. 144). It has nothing to do with a productive activity. *Phrónesis* as good sense reveals in practice what "good" means to us. It gives us a sense of justice through our own voice. Therefore, the inner and outer voice as a moral judgment would be a way to inhabit the world of teaching, taking into account its fallibility and the possibility of self-correction if one is proven wrong. The four teachers in the text display a moral attitude toward their own practice, which is closely linked with what Rousseau in *Émile* calls "the art of education":

> Therefore, when education becomes an art, it is almost impossible for it to succeed, since the conjunction of the elements necessary to its success is in no one's control. All that one can do by dint of care is to come more or less close to the goal, but to reach it requires luck. (Rousseau, 1979, p.38)

Ms. Payton is particularly concerned that her voice might not reach the students; Mr. Peters "puts a chair at his desk at the front of his room, often calling boys up for conferences"(Hansen, 1995, p. 55), and in doing so he displays what he calls a "moral stance" toward his work (Hansen, p. 56). Mr. James tries to engage with what his students are saying even if it is disruptive, while Ms. Smith no longer relies on what she calls a "cookbook" to tell her what to do. None of them follows a universalizable norm. Instead, they rely on their own perceptions of who their students are, why they struggle, how they can learn, and how closely to relate to them. Finding a resonant voice in a school environment is a way to build a moral voice of right and wrong, to become rooted, and to engender a sense of belonging.

VOICE OVER TIME (RESONANCE)

In this section, I will discuss the voice as an echo, a resonance that can exert a human effect on others over time. Hansen explores this dimension of resonance in vocation, emphasizing that vocation must "yield social values to others" (Hansen, 1995, p. 3). He also suggests that this resonance takes place across time, "through interactions with people" (Hansen, p. 4) leaving behind a trace in the future lives of the students. This is very clear to the four teachers in the book. Ms. Payton is always worried about her voice not reaching the students. As Hansen notes, she is well aware that her high expectations sometimes frustrate her more advanced students. As for Mr. Peters, he interjects, replies, gives answers, "embarking on his own search for cultural knowledge" (Hansen, p. 54) in order to better understand his students' identities and their lives. As Hansen points out, "He seeks to pay greater attention to the messages and signals boys may be sending him through their remarks and behavior" (Hansen, p. 60).

Mr. Peters is determined to establish an educational connection with his students. We can easily detect the echo of this daily work in what the students have to say about him, such as (Hansen, 1995, 60): "There must be something good if Mr. Peters sees it and believes in it" (Ibid.). Elsewhere, a boy from his class at one point says, "he's asking me to take a risk" (Hansen, p. 66). In the case of Mr. James, his constant experience of dealing with unruly or learning-disabled students gives him the courage he needs to be able to trust them. His trusting voice acts as a beacon in the difficulties he faces with his special education group. Mr. James's protective, proprietary tone—note his continual reference to "my kids"—may resonate with teachers at all levels of education: "With special students, showing that you're tuned into them and listening to their problems is number one" (Hansen, p. 77).

On her side, Ms. Smith listens to her students' voices as one would an echo. She is very attentive, and she encourages students to formulate questions and to listen to each other. Her project consists in implementing a teaching style that humanizes the individual voices of students and helps them to engage and encourage each other: "She affords students the opportunity not just to learn facts but also to think about their meaning" (Hansen, 1995, p. 98). Each of the four teachers has a vocation that feeds into their own particular sort of sensitivity toward students; they actually want to be a force for good in their lives.

In a later text, *The Moral Heart of Teaching* (2001), Hansen examines Rebecca Bushnell's (1996) study of educational practice in renaissance England, in order to discuss the notion of voice in tradition as engagement with the past. Hansen's reading of Busnhell provides teachers with a vision of the past as a voice from ancient times, an echo of what he calls "the other side" of humanist pedagogical theory and practice, far from the brutality and boredom of specific historical contexts such as "the town grammar school or the royal nursery" (Bushnell, p. 18, quoted in Hansen, 2001, p. 147). The idea of delving into the past by listening to its voice takes shape for Hansen, as he asks:

> How did Bushnell learn "to see the other side" in the first place? . . . As I understand the process, it meant letting the past speak on its own terms to her. She learned to heed the past as much as to read it. Phrased differently, she found that reading the past became a moral endeavor, as she sought to listen to the humanists without distorting their voices. (Hansen, 2001, p. 147)

"Listening without distorting their voices": this is precisely what Hansen does when he observes the four teachers in *The Call to Teach*. His stance as a "listener" is evident in that he is able to elicit frank statements from those he studies, one of them even confessing to him that:

> In the face of perceived failure, one can feel that one is "wrong," "missing something," a "bad fit" with students and with teaching itself. One can feel that one's circumstances are unfair, that one is giving but not receiving. One can feel helpless, not knowing what to do, not even knowing how to get the frustration out of mind, let alone how to resolve it in practice. As many teachers could attest, these troubling sentiments can dominate one's consciousness, even one's dreams. "Stop it!"—one cries to oneself, "stop dwelling on it!" (Hansen, 1995, p. 60)

The fact that readers can still hear this cry within is what has made Hansen's book resonate a quarter-century later. Hansen anticipates, through his unique blend of philosophical and educational research, Bushnell's later approach: engagement with the past understood from teachers' own personal stories.

I seek to recover Ms. Payton's, Mr. Peters's, Mr. James's, and Ms. Smith's voices as an echo resounding across the years. This is why "just as no two poets respond to tradition in identical ways, so no two teachers can duplicate each other's odyssey into the practice" (Hansen, 2001, p. 146). So if we are still following humanism as a kind of engagement with the past from the standpoint of the present—in a movement Gadamer calls the "fusion of horizons"—then we must take responsibility for those voices still yet to be heard, seeing "the past as estranged, yet able to illuminate present concerns" (Bushnell, 1996, p. 17, quoted in Hansen, 2001, p. 148).

Hansen grants personhood to teachers, honing in on the particular, subjective voice that not only makes each of them unique, but allows these differences to exist "among" them: "Bushnell's word choice of differences "among" people rather than between them strikes me as telling" (Hansen, 2001, p. 148).

"Telling": Agamben would say that the voice does not entirely cover the meaning and nuances of words. Words always represent an attempt to regulate the voice, whereas the voice, on her side, can make things happen beyond representation. This is precisely what Bushnell calls "the power of words":

> The humanists taught readers to see the power of words to make things happen, not just to represent the world. They may also teach us today to understand better how all texts are tied fast to both the past and the present, ever evolving and yet always rooted in their social uses and transformations. (Bushnell, 1996, p. 17, quoted in Hansen, 2001, p. 148)

From Hansen's view, Bushnell brings voices of past and present "into productive dialogue, in such a way that neither has remained the same" (Hansen, 2001, p. 149). Taking voice as a metaphor for personhood, in a dynamic and ambiguous struggle to make the words worth saying, can help us gain a broader understanding of the relevance of time's reverberation in education. It also shows us the path to humanism in the form of a renewed engagement with the past, reaching backwards from present concerns and debates. Teachers are always there, talking to students and colleagues, parents and administrators, enduring the complexity of their task and working to maintain moral coherence, with their own voice as a token of what Freire (1993) calls "conscientization" always at work in a fragile daily practice.

The voices of the four teachers in Hansen's work, thanks to his committed listening, hand down a sense of tradition in teaching. Their voices remind us that humanization is always present in the daily activity of teaching students, giving us the strength to withstand despair and hopelessness. Then an inner voice rises up and cries out, "Stop it!," and the moral heart of teaching beats once again. Therefore, the thread binding *The Call to Teach* and *The Moral Heart of Teaching* is a strong one. The continuity of the works is truly logical, because the heart is precisely what Hansen observes from the very beginning of his study of the four teachers.

So the engagement with the past in education is closely linked to the endeavor of cultivating personhood. How can teachers achieve this? They can do so through a personal commitment that allows them to speak out with an individual voice, one that goes beyond *logos* but does not lack it. What Hansen highlights in his work is that a teacher must, in the end, have a real voice and something to say if they are to engage in authentic dialogue. This relates to the possibility of becoming something other than oneself, through an endeavor to communicate and listen carefully and attentively to the voices of others. As adults, teachers can give the floor to the child hesitant to speak because nobody before had invited them to do so:

> The practice embodies a voice that can question and enlighten all who teach about what the work entails, a voice that can be discerned the moment one begins to take seriously the efforts of precursors. But it is not a voice to heed

uncritically. . . . The sense of tradition in teaching points the way to thoughtful continuity and change among past, present and future. (Hansen, 2001, p. 156)

CONCLUSION: A CALL TO POLYPHONY

Reading *The Call to Teach,* we hear a polyphony of four voices, each singing out in turn, each proving that teaching is an act of personhood and understanding, each escaping the constraints of administrative language and prescribed curricula. Teaching in this way opens a fissure in the facade of accountability and instrumental reason (Horkheimer, 2002). As in the Italo Calvino tale referenced earlier, a single voice, a song, can stand out from among other sounds to be heard, recorded, and noted. It has become a heart of flesh.

In Hansen's research, his own voice is also heard among—not between—the other voices of the teachers and their students. It is a different voice, one that can help restore a lost meaning to everyday teaching practice, marked by ambiguity and complexity. The author's voice does not drown out the others. Nevertheless, it does make its presence felt across the sentences, adjectives, and adverbs in the writing, making clear that Hansen engages in a task far beyond mere transcription. Listening to voices and writing their words takes on the character of a poetic exercise, a way to discover the vital side of the lives of teachers. Like Socrates in Plato's *Symposium* (1989), someone has to cede the floor to allow another's voice to ring out. Socrates gives the floor to Diotima, the wise woman who possesses knowledge of love, a foreign and strange character from outside the predominant scene of male philosophers, devoted to arguing among themselves and listening to their own voices. These men are not good listeners. In Cavarero's words, male philosophers are used to seeing themselves as the only makers of philosophy, which is to say they were content to close their ears to others. But Socrates is different: He dares to make room for Diotima's voice, giving her the floor in the midst of an academic debate. In other words, the true philosopher is the one who makes room for another to bring her voice to life.

In a similar way, Hansen in *The Call to Teach* plays the role of the philosopher who cedes the floor and listens carefully to other voices, and in so doing, brings them to life. Perhaps we can define philosophy as the delicate endeavor of collecting others' voices and imbuing them with life and new meaning. The history of philosophy, then, becomes a similar engagement with the past, filtering and selecting one voice over another (Nietzsche over Kierkegaard, Hegel over Kant, Arendt over Weil, and so on). But no. Maybe it is the other way around: philosophy of education seen as a path toward the recovery of small voices. Hélène Cixous, the French writer and a friend of Jacques Derrida, once said she could hear nothing but small voices whispering to her to write her books.

The Call to Teach is still calling us to listen to more than one voice, lighting a path to follow in the practice of philosophy of education today. Hansen invites us to stroll together, to listen to the sounds we take in along the way, some of them voices from afar. We can gather them together to seek answers to questions yet to be answered, or to problems we have yet to address ourselves, so as to acquire a new insight, describe a distinct knowledge, discover an unexpected truth. And then, opening our ears, we could try to listen carefully, like the king in Calvino's tale, surrendering our useless passion for accountability, control, and instrumentality, humanizing a shared experience with others, just being there, and, finally, paying attention. As Hansen says in the concluding paragraph:

> The idea of teaching as a vocation does not provide a rose-colored lens through which to perceive education. Instead, it opens a window to the range of accomplishments accessible to any serious-minded teacher. It provides a hopeful perspective that can better position teachers to take advantage of the opportunities present circumstances afford them. (Hansen, 1995, p. 161)

NOTES

1. Hansen, D. T. (2001). *Llamados a enseñar*. Barcelona: Idea Books. In this chapter, I use the English version: Hansen, D. T. (1995) *The call to teach*. Teachers College Press.
2. I feature an in-depth analysis of Agamben's contribution in my book *Cenar con Diotima: Filosofía y feminidad* (2018, pp. 263–269). Herder.

REFERENCES

Agamben, G. (2017). Experimentum vocis. In G. Agamben, *What is philosophy?* (pp. 1–28). (L. Chiesa, Trans.). Stanford University Press.

Aristotle. (trans. 1963). *Categories and de interpretatione* (J. L. Ackrill, Trans.). Clarendon Press.

Aubenque, P. (1962). *Le problème de l'être chez Aristote*. Puf.

Bushnell, R. W. (1996). *A culture of teaching: Early modern humanism in theory and practice*. Cornell University Press.

Cavarero, A. (2005). *From more than one voice. Toward a philosophy of vocal expression* (P. A. Kottman, Trans.). Stanford University Press.

Freire, P. (1993). *Pedagogy of the oppressed* (M. B. Ramos, Trans.). Continuum.

Gadamer, H.-G. (1989). *Truth and method* (J. Weinsheimer & D. G. Marshall, Trans.; 2nd rev. ed.). Continuum. (Original work published 1960)

Hansen, D. T. (1995). *The call to teach*. Teachers College Press.

Hansen, D. T. (2001). *Exploring the moral heart of teaching: Toward a teacher's creed*. Teachers College Press.

Horkheimer, M. (2002). *Crítica de la razón instrumental.* Trotta.

Kounin, J. S. (1968). *Discipline and group management in classrooms.* Holt, Rinehart, & Winston.

Lacan, J. (2004). *Le séminaire livre X: L'angoisse.* Du Seuil.

Pagès, A. (2006). *Al filo del pasado. Filosofía hermenéutica y transmisión cultural.* Herder.

Rousseau, J.-J. (1979). *Émile, or On education* (A. Bloom, Trans.). Basic Books. (Original work published 1762)

Whitaker, C. W. A. (1996). *Aristotle's De interpretation: Contradiction and dialectic.* Clarendon Press.

CHAPTER 10

Rabindranath Tagore and the Question of the Teacher's Vocation

Indrani Bhattacharjee

An enduring theme in David Hansen's thinking on education has been the constitution of attitudes that one brings, and ought to bring, to the task of educating others. Over the years, he has sharpened the idea of approaching this task aided by what he has called "a sense of vocation," through fine-grained analyses of the intellectual, moral, and aesthetic constitution of the teacher. In this paper I comment on some of the conceptual apparatus that Hansen makes use of by employing the philosophical perspective of an author who inspires some of Hansen's more recent work. I have an independent scholarly interest in the work of the Bengali poet Rabindranath Tagore (1861–1941), who set up what was in effect the first alternative school in British India. Rabindranath envisioned his educational work as one of nurturing the minds and bodies of Indian children in an environment radically opposed to that of the state schools, with their curricula designed to produce obedient subjects alienated from all ends and aspirations save those were deemed fit for them. In the year 1901, he founded the Brahmacharyashrama[1] (soon rechristened Patha Bhavana) at Santiniketan in the province of Bengal in eastern India. In what follows, I juxtapose some of Hansen's most significant claims about the teacher's vocation with some ideas drawn from Rabindranath's writings on philosophical themes, in an attempt to initiate cross-cultural dialogue on the work of teaching, its creative scope and impact. I do not expect to answer all questions that may emerge from this comparison of ideas; I may even lack the occasion to frame them all. The idea is to begin to understand the vastly different ways in which similar concerns can and do arise, and to clear a space for conversation in spite of the differences.

While poetry was the only vocation that Rabindranath ever laid claim to, he produced a great many ideas in writing. Some of these were "actionable items" (e.g., language education manuals, foundational plans for universities, and writings pertaining to "rural reconstruction" of the areas around Santiniketan). He also addressed such philosophical topics as the aims of education, the meaning of art, and the human relationship with nature. Through this second set of texts, it is possible to trace a line of thinking on what he once called "Realisation [of the self] in Action."[2] Using some of these materials, I shall produce a picture of the teacher's vocation that is broadly congenial with Hansen's. Tagore wrote a great deal on education, but I believe that to understand and evaluate these writings, it is necessary to read them against the background of his philosophical thought. Thus, all substantive claims below have been drawn from his philosophical writings.

THE TEACHER'S QUEST FOR MEANING IN THEIR WORK

What follows immediately is a reading of Hansen's views on the teacher's vocation together with some philosophical themes and assumptions that he has made his own. Among other things, I offer brief remarks on Hansen's interpretation of the cosmopolitan ideal as a mode of "responding to the world's address" to engage with its character and contents, sometimes as a teacher, and always as someone who seeks to understand one's place in it (Hansen, 2011, pp. 91–92).

Enacting a Vocation, Conduct, and Artfulness

For a student of Tagore's thought on personality (on which more below), the quest for meaning in life, and education, there is a great deal that is of interest in Hansen's empirical and scholarly studies of the constitution[3] of teachers' attitudes toward their work. Here, I draw up a small inventory of these ideas. In the following section, I comment on certain passages in Emerson's *Essays* that led me to query Hansen's account of a teacher's vocation, cantilevering the discussion toward an encounter with Tagore's view in the remainder of the paper. My reasons for making use of Emerson as a go-between will be discussed at an appropriate point in the overall argument.

Hansen's analysis of the concept of vocation begins with the claim that "[t]he sense of vocation finds its expression at the crossroads of public obligation and personal fulfillment" (Hansen, 1995, p. 3; see also p. 115). A *sense* of teaching as vocation is an understanding of one's work that yields a sense of performing a certain kind of intellectual and moral duty toward others (Hansen, pp. 123–124), as well as a sense of one's intellectual and moral growth, and the development of aesthetic responsiveness. To grasp this from a subjective perspective involves plumbing the spatial metaphor that Hansen wields: the suggestion being that the overlap between public obligation and personal fulfillment is experienced as finding oneself in a *habitation*—a metaphorical dwelling place or refuge—that preexists one's work (Hansen, pp. 14–15, 124–126; Hansen 2004a, p. 139). It is a space that one may rearrange (Hansen, 2001, pp. 122–123), producing subtle imprints of one's dwelling in it. Hansen speaks of *finding oneself* within an established practice with a history—in other words, seeing one's work as framed within a tradition of teaching-work (Hansen, 2001, p. 114ff). This way of identifying the self in the act of attending to objects and affairs in the world is emphasized by Dewey (1916), who uses it to qualify modes of engaged, creative teaching (Hansen, 2005, p. 72). Such self-identification also connotes "solicitude" toward the world, including persons and shared situations (Hansen, 2006, pp. 174–175). Equivalently, "infusion" of the self with something entails both finding a newer aspect of the self and losing an older aspect, resulting in enrichment of the meanings yielded by experiences up until that point.

All of this implies a certain open-endedness to teaching-work. Occasions for what I call *self-creation* necessarily appear in the course of events unfolding in the classroom, and hence the teacher's self gains shape as a consequence of their efforts to shape a portion of the public world. The teacher's vocation can be pictured as being akin to dwelling in a home that has an indefinite number of resources to subtly modify the inhabitant. In truth, one does not settle permanently on a way to inhabit the vocation, although to all appearances teachers *do* inhabit their vocations in specific ways. Losing and finding the self in the course of teaching happen to the extent that one freely and actively participates in teaching-learning situations. Freedom of action is a necessary condition for the creation of what Hansen calls a person's ethos, that is, "his or her characteristic conduct when in the presence of students, his or her reputation, hopes, fears or worries" (Hansen, 1995, p. 11). Now *this* is equivalent to saying that enacting a teacher's vocation implies creative engagement with teaching-work and, hence, with oneself. Dewey specifically speaks of finding oneself in one's work (Dewey, 1916). A teacher cannot find themselves in their work unless they assume autonomy to craft a way of doing things—a form of conduct, a style, even. A lack or curtailment of autonomy rules out enacting a vocation, and may in certain circumstances boil down to holding down a job, yielding little in terms of the meaning of one's work.[4]

The open-ended character of teaching-work also owes something to the *uncertainty* that accompanies it. "Uncertainty" connotes a lot of different things, both negative and positive: unplanned or unexpected turns of events (Hansen, 1995, p. 92, p. 152), a lack of sureness about one's concrete actions, their context and results (Hansen, pp. 118–119), as well as the likelihood of learning occurring at any time at all (Hansen, p. 35). It should not be supposed that enacting the teacher's vocation is a matter of privately coming to grips with the inherited and subjective meanings of teaching-work. On the contrary, one's intellectual, moral, and aesthetic growth, and repair of the self, occurs in full public view. Teachers "must render their judgments . . . before the watchful eyes of students and fellow adults, thereby revealing their moral and educational standards" (Hansen, p. 122). Sometimes things unfold in difficult circumstances, exposing individual vulnerabilities and making one's responses to a developing situation unpredictable. The peculiar irony of the metaphor of "feeling at home" in the teacher's vocation is captured well in Hansen's account of Mr. Peters's career. This teacher's commitment to his work and his desire to communicate the contents of his subject (religion) sits incongruously with the difficult circumstances of his students' lives. The highest sense of achievement that Mr. Peters reports is the realization that it is possible to "reach" his students (Hansen, pp. 56–60). Speaking metaphorically, this is akin to stepping up to the threshold of one's home to catch a glimpse of what lies within.[5]

Let us place Hansen's rendering of Dewey's notion of conduct against the backdrop of the foregoing discussion. For Hansen,

> Conduct comprises the characteristic doings of a person. In other words, it reveals and expresses his or her character. Character has to do with how the person regards and treats others. It embodies what makes the person irreproducible or noninterchangeable with others. . . . In an almost literal sense, a person materializes his or her conduct. . . . While the idea of a person helps us to understand agency—that is, the potentiality and ability to act—the idea of conduct highlights patterns of action. Conduct describes the continuity, or unity, in what a person does. (Hansen, 2001, p. 29)

Such theorizing is inspired by Dewey's attempt to "speak in the middle ground"—in this instance, between the dualism of mind and mind-external behavior.[6] Each link in a chain of acts performed by a person connects their intent with their projected aim, adding successive layers of meaning to the movement of the self toward "consummation" of the aim (Hansen, 2001, p. 29; 2006, pp. 171–172). The teacher's conduct has meaning to the extent that their individual acts add up to a chosen way of doing things in pursuance of *their* aims. Hansen asserts above that the notion of a person's character has to do with how they regard others. We sometimes tend to think of character as a private accomplishment. Yet the *ascription* of character is possible only when a person's dispositions are manifested in consistently other-regarding acts—that is, when they are assessed in the context of the person's intentional behavior around others.

In fact, we are concerned with what we call a person's character and conduct *because* they affect others favorably or adversely: This feature is what leads us to attach moral import to them. When a teacher's conduct is motivated by the aim of improving the intellectual states of their students, their activity is motivated by the desire to affect the students in a favorable way, and therefore their work necessarily has moral import. Hansen asserts that "the issue is not either/or: that teaching is an intellectual act or a moral enterprise" (Hansen, 1995, p. 123). In general, public enactment of a teacher's vocation implies heeding the imperative to be vigilant (Hansen, p. 98) concerning the intellectual and moral needs of students.

Hansen has theorized the "vigilance" aspect of teaching-work in terms of solicitude and what he has called *poesis* in teaching, that is, the ushering into life of latent words and deeds expressing the nascent intellectual, moral, and aesthetic responses of students through a quality of perception (Hansen, 2004a, pp. 135–136; 2005, pp. 66–67). I read "perception" in this context as *aisthesis*, or a keen sensory uptake, mediated by the teacher's intellectual, moral, and aesthetic sensibility. This manner of enactment of a teacher's vocation culminates in what Hansen calls, after Nehamas, an *art of living*. An art of living is a philosophical perspective on the world and the self that, among other things, calls on persons "to work on themselves," exploiting their knowledge, sensibility, and diversity of experiences "to craft a humane, meaningful life, even or especially when extant conventions seem to reject, thwart, or cheapen this project" (Hansen, 2011, pp. 32–33). Examples of individuals who sought to craft their lives in these ways include Etty Hillesum, who worked incredibly hard to provide succor and education to fellow detainees in the desperate conditions of a Nazi death camp (Hansen, 2001, p. 178ff); and Confucius, who sought to constantly cultivate humaneness through artful personal and interactive practices (Hansen, 2011, p. 23). Further illustrations in Hansen (2011) strengthen the impression that a cosmopolitan-minded educator who cultivates their intellectual, moral, and aesthetic sensibility in an attempt to live responsibly with others is Hansen's best paradigm of a teacher who enlivens their vocation.

A SKETCH OF EMERSON'S ACCOUNT OF MORAL CONDUCT

Several of Hansen's substantive claims about teaching as a vocation are shot through with an Emersonian understanding of the lot of humanity. It is evident that Hansen's philosophical trajectory passes through Emerson's world of ideas as well as Dewey's reading of Emerson, but I think that bringing the two views into closer engagement would be useful for our purposes. There are a couple of reasons for attempting this.

First, there is an aspect of Hansen's thinking on vocation that I find disquieting, and Emerson's vision shines a light on the nature of the worry. Second, in order to achieve a fruitful juxtaposition of Hansen's view with Tagore's, we need a vocabulary that has some affinity with Tagore's cache of philosophical terms. While Tagore philosophized in both Bengali and English, the central categories of his thought were developed at a time when he was working exclusively in Bengali.[7] But the difficulty of conducting a cross-cultural dialogue is not just linguistic, but also conceptual: I wish to present Tagore's views in a language that isn't weighed down by unfamiliar metaphysical assumptions, without denying the salience of those assumptions for his thought. Emerson's prose is replete with philosophical notions, several of which find resonance in Tagore's thought.[8] In particular, Tagore's complex ideas about the relationship of human beings to their work become easier to appreciate once we have attended closely to the implications of the Emersonian concepts of reception and aversion.

Reception is the Emersonian theme that Hansen explicitly develops in his writings (e.g., 2006, pp. 168–169). In "Experience," Emerson brings up reception in the context of his arresting remarks on the "evanescence and lubricity" of the things of experience, noting that even calamitous events deliver no lasting truth or wisdom. The death of his son 2 years previously now strikes him as the loss of "a beautiful estate"; he finds that he cannot "get it closer to [himself]" (Emerson, 2000, p. 309). Similarly, the stories and great ideas that we are so excited by inevitably fade away to the obscure regions of our minds; in short, "Life is not worth the taking, to do tricks in" (Emerson, p. 313). In such lines, Emerson captures most palpably the sense of not really "getting" the understanding that we seek in exchange for going through life—"not a berry for our philosophy," as he puts it. As Hansen interprets the italicized lines below, nor do we "get" the goods that are said to make our lives meaningful—love, education, and so forth. Emerson remarks: "*All I know is reception; I am and I have: but I do not get,* and when I have fancied I have gotten anything, I found I did not. I worship with wonder the great Fortune. My *reception* has been so large that I am not annoyed by receiving this or that superabundantly" (Emerson, p. 325; emphasis added).

We do not get, but we may *have* a great deal if we "dwell in the receptive mode," as Hansen puts it. We may come to *have* moral, intellectual, and aesthetic sensibility and the ability to perceive keenly as features of our character (Hansen, 2006, p. 169). Emerson explains how: "We live amid surfaces, and the true art of life is to skate well on them" (2000, p. 314). This remark helps us to gloss Hansen's proposed ideal of *tenacious humility.* Tenacious humility is a compound virtue: *tenacity* connotes "staying the course" or consistently making efforts to bring about intellectual and moral growth in one's students, whereas *humility* is about treating them as moral beings in Kant's sense while being accepting of personal differences, institutional constraints, and so on (Hansen, 2001, p. 167). For Emerson, to be tenacious is to value the calling of the present moment: "Since our office is with moments, let us husband them. . . . Let us be poised, and wise, and our own, to-day" (Emerson, 2000, p. 314). We know only that an attitude of reception is called for, an attitude that can coexist with being moved to respond to the world through action. We must act "artfully," that is, skillfully and in "our own" ways, knowing that our actions are all we *have* in the moment. Crucially, the upshot of artfully executed action is yet more *having*: when we are in the receptive mode, we *have* out of all proportion to how much we put into our work: "The benefit overran the merit the first day, and has overrun the merit ever since" (Emerson, p. 326). This predicament calls for humility, or *grace.* Emerson's remark about "skating well" suggests that the attitude of accepting what one *has* involves grace. Graceful conduct is a matter of *habitually* "skating well": in other words, artful living is a practice that does not end at the classroom door. *Maintaining* the self in a receptive attitude, whether one is attending to the world or to oneself, is constitutive of Emerson's idea of practical wisdom.

The Emersonian perspective gives us an account of why approaching teaching-work as a vocation—that is, as characterized by receptivity— provides personal fulfillment. Hansen emphasizes Dewey's belief that the purpose of an instance of teaching is not to accomplish learning, but to engage students in activities in an environment created to facilitate teaching and learning (Hansen, 2001, p. 75, p. 85, and *passim*). Emerson helps us to understand why instances of engrossing, "object-directed" rather than "self-directed" teaching are fulfilling; he also describes a mode of being and acting that brings about fulfillment. Looking to "get" results—for example, executing a complete lesson plan; communicating the two key concepts around which one's lesson was organized—blocks out all that one can *have* by "husbanding the moment" when serving one's students.

A complementary idea in Emerson's thought is that of aversion. It is not an idea that Hansen puts to work, but it seems to me that it is presupposed by his account of a teacher attending to their calling. *Aversion* is the descriptor that Emerson uses for the opposite tendency to conformism, namely, self-reliance. Nonconformism might seem at odds with being receptive to the world: It is not immediately clear how one might have an intense engagement with the social world by means of teaching, and yet avert one's eye from, say, the traditions that undergird the work. However, aversion does not entail either wholesale rejection of the social realm or a radical Nietzschean fix to a world bereft of genuine values. I would argue that aversion makes possible distinct enactments of the vocation of teaching, through eliciting an authentic quest for the self.[9] It is hard to see how teachers would find *themselves* in their work without enacting aversion, however subtly. Someone might efficiently occupy roles and execute all manner of functions, but as Emerson remarks, these are just so many "screens" that obfuscate their personal character. "But do your work, and I shall know you. Do your work, *and you shall reinforce yourself*" (Emerson, 2000, pp. 136–137, emphasis added). One catches a glimpse of Dewey's self-creating, world- or work-infused self in Emerson's account of attending to one's vocation.

Are the requirements of aversion too strong for Hansen's purposes? Surely one has met teachers who evince a sense of vocation but come across as "regular folk." They do not seem especially nonconformist, and do not evince anything like an authentic quest for the self. Hansen, too, provides examples of teachers who do not feel at home in their vocation and do not present with especially heroic enactments of it. In response, one can point out that an authentic quest for meaning in one's work need not have a strong outward expression. Emerson holds that "the great man is he who in the midst of the crowd keeps with perfect sweetness the independence of solitude" (Emerson, p. 137), where "sweetness" connotes both poise in aversion and solicitous regard for the other.[10] Such an attitude implies an ongoing concern with the self.

It is now possible to articulate my sense of unease with Hansen's account of teaching as vocation. In his first two books, he does not theorize nearly enough about the ways in which the work of teaching and the enlivening of a teaching philosophy, or more generally, an art of living, transforms one's character. There may be a certain overemphasis on receptivity in the previous works—which, I suspect, is not enough to prepare us for the quality of aversion in such cosmopolitan-minded teachers as Diogenes, Confucius, Montaigne, and Tagore. However, it seems to me that aversion characterizes the conduct of a Diogenes as much as it does that of a Mrs. Payton: They both express aversion in the sense that their work forms an element in a carefully crafted ethos. I would argue that aversion is a characteristic feature of the conduct of a teacher enlivening her vocation. Hansen stresses the irreplaceability of the individual who performs teaching-work with a sense of vocation; on the present view, one cannot begin to explain this phenomenon without recourse to the condition that makes it possible.

RABINDRANATH TAGORE'S VIEW OF HUMAN NATURE

My concern with aversion above stems from a Tagorean view of the phenomenon. To understand that view, it is necessary to make a foray into the perspective on human nature that undergirds Rabindranath's educational philosophy. The ideas present in the next section are defended in Tagore (2008), although they are foreshadowed in both Tagore (2004) and *Śāntiniketan (SN)*.

The Quest for the Universal

The most important constituent of human nature for Rabindranath is what he calls the "luminous imagination" (Tagore, 2008, p. 14). Among its several functions is that of envisioning a "wholeness" or unity of things that induces the self to aspire more or less consciously toward an ideal of "perfection." To appreciate what that means, one needs to understand the role of the imagination in what I will call self-creation. We sometimes speak of people "reinventing" themselves when they make noticeable changes in their lives, e.g., when they freely switch trades or programs of study, or reorganize their social lives, commitments, interests, or looks. For Rabindranath, the impulse that drives this change is a constant feature of the self. It is the impulse to break through the categories in terms of which one understands one's capacities and dispositions to newer self-configurations via fresh ideas and projects. The imagination fuels the process by envisioning new projects to nurture. Crucially, the luminous imagination serves no practical purpose beyond expressing one's creative potential in this sense. For this reason, Rabindranath describes it as a "superfluous" feature of the mind.

Let us break this down using an illustration. Consider a computer programmer—let's call her Iman—who ceases to see herself as a tech person, and plans to use her savings to get trained in the Montessori method. She is drawn to the idea of educating young children, and looks forward to trading ideas with other similarly creative, social beings. Notice that wants and goals are themselves fruits of imaginative projection. Becoming an early childhood educator is not necessary for biological survival; it is an imaginatively projected goal, whose attainment involves exercising capacities that one either has or is willing to develop. Sometimes, in order to satisfy our projected goals, we are prepared to forego a great deal. We readily organize our other desires, prioritizing some and suppressing others (SN, VI: 2) by acts of will; the weighing of priorities also involves imaginative projection. For example, Iman might forego a vacation and work overtime to fund her education. Using a logical trope common to teleological models, Rabindranath says that a person's imagined future selves motivate her conduct in the present, modifying the meanings of her individual actions and their results, causing her to plumb possibly hidden reservoirs of energy and recalibrate her desires, beliefs, and schemes. While the call that Iman answers has a point of reference in the external world, it has the form of an imaginative self-presentation.

The framework of ideas from which Rabindranath draws his view of the imagination is Advaita Vedānta, a family of idealist philosophies, all members of which posit a unitary ontological real, conventionally labelled as *brahman*. Rabindranath's family was deeply invested in the Brahmo Samaj, a reformist religious group constituted in 19th-century Bengal that adopted a roughly non-dualistic reading of the Upaniṣads as its creed, with brahman doing double duty as personal God. Rabindranath himself claimed to have a poetical vision of his faith, which led him to regard brahman as manifested in the diversity of perceptible forms, including persons. From the idea of a limited manifestation of divinity in persons he drew the implication that humanity was the locus of potentially infinite perfection. This intuition underwrites the nature and content of his educational thought.

Temperament-wise, Rabindranath alternated between Advaitism and the dualism of self and the world. His reception of both physical nature and humanity appears to have been especially keen, going by his own account (Tagore, 2004, pp. 15, 54–55) and the evidence of his art. Recognizing the role that his own education (which occurred at home) had played in developing his sensibilities, he maintained that while the capacity for empathy was universal, it required nurturing. "Children," he writes, "with the freshness of their senses come directly to the intimacy of this world. This is the

first great gift they have. They must . . . never again lose their power of immediate communication with it" (Tagore, p. 96). This idea of "intimacy"[11]
is pivotal to all aspects of Rabindranath's thought. In *SN* IV: 2, Rabindranath
makes an interesting argument about the consequences of denying the metaphysical unity underlying the experience of intimacy:

> Those who are united at the root, not only come to be different from one an-
> other when the fundamental unity is excised, they come to oppose one another.
> Those who abide in intimacy due to the un-complex tie of a fundamental unity
> are drawn to mutual destruction when separated.

Rabindranath here affirms that there is something *right* about the sense
of unmediated intimacy with the other, on the assumption that unity that
underwrites that experience manifests as *harmony* and *universal beneficence*.[12] Intimacy manifests as moral harmony and goodwill when it occurs
in social relations. It manifests as aesthetic experience when one has a sense
of communion with nature, a piece of art, or a subject of study. As for the
human relationship with the natural environment, the ills of denying our
intimacy with it are starkly evident today. The lack of intimacy accounts for
a great many things, including the blunting of children's sensibilities toward
academic subjects that appear alien thanks to unsympathetic curriculum
design and soulless pedagogy.

Rabindranath argues that the realization of one's unity with the world
is the ultimate goal of human action. This is not to say that one always has,
or ought to have, the ultimate goal in view. What one ordinarily has is a
drive to continually transcend the limits of one's personality through the
imaginative projection of new goals and undertakings. Humans typically ra-
tionalize these novel undertakings as quests for "deeper meaning" (Tagore,
2008, p. 113). Rabindranath renders the drive toward self-transcendence as
a quest for perfection (Tagore, 2004, p. 291).[13] The imagination, he says,
can sometimes envision perfection as that which gives a unified meaning to
all human efforts. It arouses in our minds "the sense of perfection which
is our true sense of morality." These imaginative interventions are special
because they result in creative works of great scope—"those creations . . .
that reveal the divinity in him—which is his humanity—in the varied manifestations of truth, goodness and beauty, in the freedom of activity which is
not for his use but for his ultimate expression" (Tagore, 2008, pp. 14–15).
There can, of course, be creations of smaller scope also: The reader will
recall Iman seeking to transcend the circle of her current self by discovering
a newer expression of her personality. Rabindranath does not state a norm
by which the improvement or degree of perfection of human nature is to be
judged: That is, he is not concerned with *perfecting* human nature. Instead,
his educational efforts are focused on nurturing what we might call limited
or intermediate *perfections*.

Rabindranath emphasizes that there is no special *method* involved in seeking perfection(s): "Every true freedom that we may attain in any direction broadens our path of self-realization, which is in superseding the self" (Tagore, 2008, p. 34). This claim together with the longish sentence quoted directly above implies that we misapprehend our gains when we think that we have *gotten* something, for example, riches, a good reputation as a teacher, the love of our life, and so on. The conviction that one has gotten something spells the death of the human spirit, whose dharma, or rightful nature—what Rabindranath calls its "religion"—is to continually surpass present limits. The aspiration for perfection is expressed in the drive toward self-transcendence, *not* self-aggrandizement (Tagore, 2004, p. 307; *SN*, I: 4).

THE INDIVIDUAL AND THEIR WORLD

Thus far we have seen how Rabindranath regarded the pursuit of self-transcendence as the universal human vocation, and had a glimpse or two of the art of living associated with that view. In this section, we focus on his conception of individuality or "personality," and a fuller account of the contribution of the imagination toward creating both the self and the world that forms its habitation.

In Tagore (2004), there is a discussion on the perceived value of individuality. He describes individuality as being indubitably real, unique, and incomparable in value; to preserve it, we are prepared to forego comforts, face off near-impossible odds, and perform blindingly selfish acts. Since individuality is a manifestation of the ontological unity, its erasure by conformity or repression results quite literally in an irreplaceable loss to the world. But these claims only serve to raise the question of the purpose of preserving individuality: in other words, *why* do we follow our dreams, pursue vocations and avocations of our choice, and painstakingly craft our lives according to uniquely individual plans? Do our self-regarding behaviors point beyond the self? Rabindranath reasons that humans would not seek to preserve their individuality if doing so did not promise a larger payoff. This payoff, he suggests, is realizing the potential of the self for "fullness" (Tagore, p. 306), or "wholeness." The attainment of wholeness is associated with what he calls "joy" (*ānanda*).

Commenting on one of his favorite Upaniṣadic verses,[14] Rabindranath writes that those who have achieved the fullest expression of their individualities through actions, knowledge, and loving relationships—the spiritually adept—find themselves to be infused with the world—with "[t]he joy of the sunlight, the joy of the free air, mingling with the joy of their lives" (Tagore, 2004, p. 327). Non-adepts have a measure of this joy whenever the imagination awakens to meaningful and pleasant surroundings. Rabindranath suggests that human beings are fundamentally artists; that in order to attain distinctiveness of personality (i.e., specific intellectual, moral, and aesthetic dispositions), we require generous stimulation from the world. Sans such intimate contact with, and opportunities for imaginative assimilation of the world, "we become vague to ourselves." Moreover, our individual personalities grow in scope "with a larger and deeper experience of our personal self *in our own universe* through sympathy and imagination" (Tagore, 2008, p. 75; emphasis added). Each of us dwells in a world modified, or made "real" to us by the imagination: As Rabindranath puts it, we are "naturally indifferent to things that merely exist," and seek to inhabit a world of things and persons that we have an interest in and care about. The imagination, which actively inflects our cognitive uptake of the world, also projects the ideal, value-filled world of objects and relationships in which we dwell and work (Tagore, 2008, p. 76).

CONCLUSION: A TAGOREAN VIEW OF THE TEACHER'S VOCATION

The preceding discussion serves to accentuate the ever-present "address of the world" out of which emerge calls specific to the many dimensions of perfection in a person's life. Given that self-transcendence is the ruling idea here, we are not restricted to the idea of a life built around a single vocation. Rabindranath described his own motivation to teach in vocational terms, saying that teaching offered a route to "self-realization in the life of Man through . . . disinterested service" (Tagore, 2008, p. 92). Teaching is "disinterested service" to the extent that it is a means for self-transcendence, as opposed to self-aggrandizement in the Emersonian sense explored above.[15]

Rabindranath's views tend to stretch the concept of vocation itself by adding to it a dimension of creativity, while also bringing into its ambit work done under different manifestations of personality. Perhaps the reader wonders how Rabindranath's thought helps with the question of the "valuation" of such work, given that it appears to have greater subjective meaning than objective worth. This is not a new question for anyone theorizing on, for example, teaching as a vocation. Perhaps one way to counter the specious arguments that creative vocations in general serve no purpose for the public is to develop in detail the perspective on work that Rabindranath outlines.

Take teaching as a vocation. Rabindranath enjoins *intimacy* as the core of all work with students. This accounts for his injunctions about the cultivation of an attitude of care in teachers: devoting mind and spirit to the service of students, animating their interests and desire to know, and extending to them "affection" or solicitude (O'Connell, 2012, p. 203). According to this picture, on the one hand, work is expression of one's personality in pursuit of self-transcendence; on the other hand, teaching-work by definition involves receptivity, and making intimately "real" one's students and their needs and the subject being taught. In concrete terms, this can mean consciously stepping away from one's preferred pedagogical methods in order to address an emergent learning need, and consequently finding oneself in communion with one's students over a subject. Outside the classroom, it can mean showing solicitous regard to a student who expresses hurt or displeasure at one's failure to sufficiently appreciate their efforts at learning, and consequently learning something valuable about one's ethos as a teacher.

The most powerful part of this vision of teaching, in my view, is the continuity of the teaching-learning environment with the teacher's ethos.[16] The Tagorean perspective shines a light on the symbiotic relationship between teachers and students. Students are elements of the environment created by the teacher, and are instrumental in giving definition to the teacher's creative personality. Conversely, the teacher's ministrations help the student's self-creation and manifestations of personality. Here we have an alternative picture of the work of teaching in need of wider and deeper articulation. Once that is accomplished, one can raise afresh the question of the "valuation" of creative work of this order.

NOTES

1. The definite article before *Brahmacharyashrama* indicates a definite description of the institution in question. In Hindu ethics, *brahmacarya* describes the first of four (sometimes three) stages of life, during which one gets an education substantial enough to negotiate the remainder of one's days. An interpretation of these can be found in the essay "The Four Stages of Life," in Tagore (2008). Tagore initially conceived of his school as a creative interpretation of the classical ideal. The school soon lost its revivalist feel, however, for a variety of reasons. See O'Connell (2012), Chapter 3.

2. This is the title of one of Tagore's London lectures from 1913. This lecture and other kindred pieces written for American and British audiences are collected in Tagore (2004).

3. I use the term *constitution* more or less in Emerson's sense. See, for example, "Self-Reliance," in Emerson (2000, p. 135) and a related use in "The Over-Soul," p. 243.

4. The concern for grasping, making, and disclosing the meaningfulness of the work of teaching is explored in greater detail in Hansen (2004a), by means of the notion of a *poetics* of teaching.

5. No doubt some people dwell uncomfortably in their homes or home countries. This analogy with a tenuous sense of belonging or citizenship is significant in view of Hansen's preferred rendering of *kosmopolites* as "inhabitant of the world" over "citizen of the world." The preferred rendering may be "closer to the teacher," as Hansen argues (2011, p. 46), but it lacks the connotation of a rightful claim to the world. A cosmopolitan educator can and often does stake such a claim through their work and vision of the world.

6. Saito describes Dewey's quest for the "continuous regeneration of a moving middle in an ongoing transaction between [opposing and] ever-changing factors." Dewey's conceptions of conduct and self are examples of such "transactional" constructs (Saito, 2005, p. 72).

7. Rabindranath produced the *Śantiniketan (SN)* lectures and essays between 1908 and 1914. During this period, he made the first sustained effort to articulate his philosophical and religious commitments in writing. This period in Rabindranath's literary career is called "the Gitanjali Phase," since it is when he produced the four books of poetry that served as sourcebooks for the English text of *Gitanjali*. The poetry in these books has a strong metaphysical and spiritual bent, and as a result, so does *Gitanjali*. It is no coincidence that *Śantiniketan* contains meditations in prose on several ideas that also appear in poetical garb. Sometimes Rabindranath interprets his own poetry for the benefit of an audience—for example, *SN*, VII: 4 contains a philosophical interpretation of the poem *Sonār tarī* (translated by Alam as "The Golden Boat"; see *The Essential Tagore (ET)*, p. 228)—but often it is not clear in what shape an idea first appeared to him. Some readings of Rabindranath's poetry from the Gitanjali Phase ignore the fact that it emerged in his unfolding philosophical and spiritual life. I suppose this is an extreme reaction to Western attributions of a wishy-washy, "oriental mysticism" to Tagore: The reader may refer to Aronson (1978) for some particularly vitriolic Western reactions to the poems. Unfortunately, this strategy of avoidance leads to serious under-interpretation; see, for example, Amit Chaudhuri's remarks on the poem/song that he translates as "To the festival of creation I have an invitation," in his "Introduction" to *ET*, pp. xxvi–xxvii. I am no literary critic, and am not concerned with the question of latitude in interpretation of poetry. But *if* one treats verses as philosophical texts—and sometimes there are excellent grounds for doing so—then the possibility of misinterpretation becomes real.

I have used the format *title, chapter, numbered essay* when citing the text of *Śantiniketan*. For example, *SN* (I: 12) refers to the essay titled *Prārthanā*. The essays *aren't* numbered in the text, which makes it inconvenient to refer to them in English. Translations from this text are mine. The reader will note that I use the poet's first name to refer to him; for a speaker of Bengali to do otherwise is a tad unnatural.

8. It is possible to find resonances between Rabindranath's thought and Emerson's Transcendentalism, given the relationship of both to the philosophy of the Upaniṣads, and between Rabindranath's official faith of Brahmoism and Unitarianism. Rabindranath even composed songs for the Unitarian hymnal (Chattopadhyay, 2018). In 1912, he gave some lectures at the Unitarian Chapel and Unity Club at Urbana, Illinois, at the request of a local minister. These lectures and some others given at Harvard and London in 2012–13 are included in Tagore (2004); a single lecture is included in *ET* (Tagore, p. 145ff). Krishna Kripalani, Rabindranath's biographer in English, appears somewhat embarrassed by these pieces. "Profound and beautiful are these thoughts," he remarks, "and yet one cannot help wondering what made him dole out this characteristically Tagorean blend of poetizing, philosophizing and sermonizing to his American audience. Did the Boston Brahmins recall the Emersonian flavor in them?" (Kripalani, 2012, p. 209). I myself am happy to use any relevant similarities between the two thinkers that suit my present purposes. I also happen to think that engaging with Rabindranath makes it possible to appreciate Emerson's thought independently of the presumption that its influence on American individualism, democracy, and pragmatism are its strongest suit.

Kripalani's discomfort with Rabindranath's sermonizing to the Americans echoes the bewilderment expressed in the American press back in 1912 (see *ET*, p. 13). But there are commentators today who think that a reevaluation of Rabindranath's philosophical prose is in order. For example, Sen Gupta (2005, p. 8) invokes Heidegger to defend his philosophical style, recalling that Heidegger detected in Hölderlin's writings a "disclosive or 'originative,' poetic mode of thinking"—a mode of thinking that he thought was necessary to reanimate. Sen Gupta notes that Rabindranath's biggest philosophical debt was to the Upaniṣads. What that means is that the debt extends to modes of thinking and experience as well: The "world-disclosing" character of the Principal Upaniṣads is a combined effect of all three elements that Kripalani mentions in the remark above.

9. Emerson talks in terms of uniqueness rather than authenticity (e.g., p. 150). Emerson's own career as a minister is a fine example of enacting a vocation in aversive mode.

10. In "The Over-Soul," Emerson makes it clear that the aversive self-reliant individual is inherently social: "More and more the surges of everlasting nature enter into me, and I become public and human in my regards and actions" (Emerson, p. 250). There is no space here to discuss the transcendentalist import of this claim; I will only note that this is a remarkably Tagorean thing to say.

11. *Ātmīyatā* in Bengali (*SN* I: 4; IV: 6, etc.). *Ātmīya* literally means "of the self."

12. "Harmony" and "universal beneficence" are my renderings of *śāntaṃ* and *śivaṃ*, respectively. See also S. Tagore's reading of the ideal as "unity in harmony" (2003, pp. 81–82).

13. The term used by him is "the All"—an awkward rendering of the Upanishadic term *bhūmā* (see, e.g., *SN*, VII: 14; XI: 2), which Olivelle translates as "plenitude" (1996, p. 165). However, Rabindranath does not read the relevant verse quite as Olivelle does, so I have settled for "the Universal," which retains the sense of "the All," while being somewhat easier on the ear.

14. *Īśā*, 2. See Olivelle (1996, p. 249).

15. The context of Rabindranath's remark makes it clear that this is indeed what he meant by "disinterested service."

16. A full account of Rabindranath's view on this matter would require commentary on the *tapovana* (roughly, "forest retreat with teachers") model that served as the inspiration for his school. The reader is referred to O'Connell (2012) for details.

REFERENCES

Aronson, A. (1978). *Rabindranath through Western eyes*. Ṛddhi-India. (Original work published 1943)

Chattopadhyay, S. S. (2018). "New light on Tagore," *Frontline* magazine. https://frontline.thehindu.com/arts-and-culture/new-light-on-tagore/article10106610.ece

Dewey, J. (1916). *Democracy and education*. Macmillan Company.

Emerson, R. W. (2000). *The essential writings of Ralph Waldo Emerson*, B. Atkinson (Ed.). Random House, The Modern Library.

Hansen, D. T. (1995). *The call to teach*. Teachers College Press.

Hansen, D. T. (2001). *Exploring the moral heart of teaching: Toward a teacher's creed*. Teachers College Press.

Hansen, D. T. (2004a). A poetics of teaching. *Educational Theory, 54*(2), 119–142.

Hansen, D. T. (2004b). John Dewey's call for meaning. *Education and Culture, 20*(2), 7–24.

Hansen, D. T. (2005). Creativity in teaching and building a meaningful life as a teacher. *Journal of Aesthetic Education, 39*(2), 57–68.

Hansen, D. T. (2006). Dewey's book of the moral self. In D. T. Hansen (Ed.), *John Dewey and our educational prospect: A critical engagement with Dewey's Democracy and education* (pp. 165–187). State University of New York Press.

Hansen, D. T. (2011). *The teacher and the world: A study of cosmopolitanism as education*. Routledge.

Kripalani, K. (2012). *Rabindranath Tagore: A biography*. Visva-Bharati Press. (Original work published 1960)

O'Connell, K. M. (2012). *Rabindranath Tagore: The poet as educator*. Visva-Bharati Press.

Olivelle, P. (1996). *Upaniṣads*. Oxford University Press.

Saito, N. (2005). *The gleam of light: Moral perfectionism and education in Dewey and Emerson*. Fordham University Press.

Sen Gupta, K. (2005). *The philosophy of Rabindranath Tagore*. Ashgate Publishing Limited.

Tagore, R. (2004). Sādhanā: The realisation of life. In S. K. Das (Ed.), *The English writings of Rabindranath Tagore, Vol. 2*. Sahitya Akademi. (Original work published 1913)

Tagore, R. (2008). *The religion of man*. Visva-Bharati Press. (Original work published 1931)

CHAPTER 11

Sharing Sebold (and So Much More)

Caroline Heller

"The witness attempts to (be)hold them care-fully, not by setting them in amber or pinning them to a wall, but rather through buoyant, flexible prose that nonetheless (ideally) possesses the strength of silk."

(Hansen, 2017, p. 29)

David Hansen and I were colleagues for 8 years in the College of Education at the University of Illinois, Chicago. We both taught aspiring classroom teachers. I arrived at UIC in 1993, a few years after David. It was my first tenure-track job, and, like David, I hoped to commit my professional life to teaching and research, though I was also wary of the potential of research to reduce rather than illuminate the infinitely complex processes of educating and being educated. I arrived to UIC much troubled by the Western premise that scientific theories (or in the case of educational research, social scientific theories) stand as grand "truths," while stories of everyday lives—teachers' and children's lives in classrooms, for instance—tend to be received as unreliable folktales, devoid of scholarly import. As a doctoral student, I'd pinned words above my computer (I've long forgotten the source): *A fine teacher is a fine teacher no matter what educational theories she might suffer from.* I shared this line with David when we met over lunch early in my first semester at UIC. I remember how good it felt to laugh with David and how wondrous it was to poke fun at ourselves, knowing that it didn't diminish our commitment to our field.

I was young(ish) and starting to discover some semblance of my strengths and character as a researcher and teacher; to meet a kindred spirit like David felt extraordinary. In each other's company we worked to become our own brand of researcher and most importantly, the kind of teacher each of us aspired to be. Neither of us felt that we understood the why or how of successful teaching, though we were overwhelmed with joy when our classes went well. From the get-go, my friendship with David seemed to allow for permissions that generally take time to earn. For instance, however much we longed to be good teachers, if either of us felt *too* successful, we properly reminded the other that in the spirit of our growth it was likely time for us to fall on our faces.

David, his wife, Elaine Fuchs, my wife, Eileen Ball, and I shared many meals during those UIC years. Our favorite meeting place was a cavernous restaurant in Chinatown where the curtained booths and generous wait staff invited us to linger for hours, learning about each other's lives, our families, sharing our work, our dreams. It was a time when the language of accountability was starting to dominate educational discourse. We consoled each other with our shared worry that teachers—aspiring ones and veteran teachers alike—were being forced more and more to satisfy the purposes of policymakers and testing companies, vital energy pulled from their central motivation—*teaching*.

And we talked about books and the reading life that David's mother Anne had long ago ignited in him. He introduced me to the many writers who had guided him—writers as diverse as Phillip Jackson, Michel de Montaigne, George Eliot, Alasdair MacIntyre, Stanley Cavell, Iris Murdoch, Sandra Harding, Jean Bethke Elshtain, Michio Takeyama.

My years at UIC, when David's office was just down the hall from mine, made me wiser and more at home in the world—the academic one and the real one—because David Hansen was nearby.

When we all left Chicago, I had little idea that the days yet to come would only strengthen our bonds.

David left Chicago to take his position as director of the Philosophy and Education Program at Teachers College in New York City (Elaine, a renowned cell biologist, soon followed, becoming professor and researcher at Rockefeller University) the same year Eileen and I left Chicago to take teaching positions near Boston. We began our new positions in September 2001.

While none of us directly witnessed the devastating moments of that day, 9/11 changed us and we drew our only real sustenance from experiencing that sense of change collectively. To add to my own dazed state, my father died a week later, and my disorientation—ranging from feeling numb to feeling crushed—increased exponentially after losing him.

All this brings me to October 15, 2001. I learned that W. G. Sebald, whose books *The Emigrants* and *Rings of Saturn* I'd read and cherished, would be reading at NYC's 92nd Street Y, introduced by Susan Sontag. In Boston, Eileen and I boarded a nearly empty train bound for NYC. David, an admirer of Sontag, but who hadn't yet discovered Sebald's work, met us, and we entered the auditorium where the reading was held.

Sebald read from his new book *Austerlitz*, about a man who spent his life feeling that something in his soul had been irretrievably lost. When he was 4 years old, just before Hitler marched into Prague, the family's homeland for many generations, his parents had put him on a Kindertransport train. Alone, the little boy arrived in England, picked up by the foster parents who would raise him in Wales and rename him, never telling him about his origins, who he really was. Now in his sixties, Jacques has set about to search for his identity. He travels many places and ends up in Marienbad, Czechoslovakia, because he learned that just before Hitler transformed their world, his biological parents had traveled there with him for a brief vacation.

W. G. Sebald, tall and dignified, with a grey mustache and thinning white hair, read from *Austerlitz* with enormous feeling, breaking up the sadness of the story with moments of humor, his face sometimes breaking into a shy grin.

I jotted words and phrases on my program, putting an exclamation point by a line that Sebald read especially slowly, pausing and looking up, as though he himself were newly astonished by the revelation: *At some time in the past, Austerlitz thought, I must have made a mistake and now I am living the wrong life.*

On several occasions during the reading I peeked at David, sitting to my right. Each time my peek found him leaning forward in his seat, a meditative look on his face, as if intent on catching not just every word, but every gesture, every nuance. David looked mesmerized, as though in Sebald's presence, he had both found and *been* found. While peeking at my friend, I regaled in the feeling that after all the writers David had introduced me to, I had finally given him a needed treasure in return.

As Sebald read I felt from him a sense of all of our communal woundedness at that moment—certainly my own. Just as I had not directly witnessed the terror of 9/11, I had not witnessed the era that had formed my own Holocaust survivor parents. Sebald's words, depicting Jacques's sense of loss and longing, filled me with grief and connection to them, something I so yearned to fully feel at that time.

All of Sebald's books are about people we first believe escaped destruction because they *survived*. But through faint hints that build on one another, we realize that the people Sebald writes about, people like Jacques Austerlitz, who accessed "safety" before the genocide reached its full measure, were shattered in other ways, a different devastation from those murdered or imprisoned in concentration camps. They lived with a bone-and-marrow-deep feeling that there was a life essence that they had never been able to gather into themselves, that they were not quite fully alive. Decades after their exiles from their homelands, Sebald's people—and Jacques Austerlitz is one of many whose lives Sebald imagines and renders—descend into an overwhelming exhaustion. Sebald sets about to trace the routes of their exiles from their homelands, and in his search, he seems to inherit their losses, their displacement, their longings. Each layer of his text deepens his relationship with the people whose lives he imagines and narrates almost simultaneously, achieving a level of profound intimacy, of parallel journey and solidarity.

After our evening with Sebald, even amidst the suffering of his people and the suffering of 9/11, we wandered NYC feeling newly and uncannily receptive and alive.

Unbeknownst to me, for weeks after that evening, David returned to the 92nd St. Y to listen to Sebald's words, which the Y had archived. Day after day, he walked from his home on East 63rd to the Upper East Side, where he sat alone in the Y archives, filling notebook upon notebook with commentary and appreciation of Sebald's unique mode of remembrance, which a reviewer of Sebald's work once described as prose that seems to be "narrated by something like a timeless, sentient cloud" (*New York Times*, Feb. 9, 2014; John Williams). Only later did I learn from David that he was not just revisiting our evening, he was there to study, to absorb Sebald's method of remembrance and representation by listening to his words again and again. "Sebald is excessively concerned not to trespass wrongfully," David would later write. "He does not explain what he sees, but rather presents things in such a way that understanding can emerge if one is attentive" (Hansen, 2012a, p. 128).

Over time, David quietly developed a seminar for his doctoral students at Teachers College based on close reading of Sebald's books. He aimed to link Sebald's work of remembrance to theirs as students of education. His excitement about his newly created seminar shined fully in an email he wrote to me when the seminar ended. "Here are scanned pages of a volume of *The Emigrants* that my students and I used. All of us became wonderfully involved in reading Sebald word-by-word. At the close of the course, I passed our in-class volume around the room and asked each student to write a paragraph in response to the book. I wrote one too. At the end I passed the book around and asked each person to read one of their peers' entries. In some ways, my students' words are as haunting and evocative to me as those of the beautiful author they read together" (Hansen, 2012b).

One reflection in particular gave me a window on what David's seminar had inspired in his students. "Immersing myself in this elegiac text," a young man named Robert wrote, "surrounded by the echoing dialogue of my peers these past weeks, has worked a deep action upon my heart. Memories, once silent and static, now force their way forward through my waking thoughts. Memories of my life, but also the weighted past of others, now seem woven into my concerns and actions. I cannot just act. I must also remember" (Hansen, 2012b).

Shortly after teaching this seminar, David completed a new essay, which he titled, "W. G. Sebald and the Tasks of Ethical and Moral Remembrance."

"W. G. Sebald undertook a profound inquiry into the possibility of a formative human relation with difficult legacies from the past," David began. "I also hope to contribute to an emerging literature in our field that addresses questions of historical consciousness, remembrance, and education." He goes on: "If moral remembrance has to do with how, in interaction with others, I respond to a collective past in which I am implicated, ethical remembrance denotes the process of getting there" (Hansen, 2012a, p. 125).

In the essay, David analyzes Sebald's writing, and in doing so seems to recognize new aspects of his own quest to adequately represent the work of teachers, including the immense challenge of traversing the muck and muddle of grammar, syntax, semantics—to find words that feel true. "The reader witnesses the narrator struggling with how to describe justly what he sees, hears, and reads. The narrator sometimes feels his sensibility compressed, flattened, and emptied out the moment he begins to enunciate himself" (Hansen, 2012a, p. 127). And David goes on in the essay to ask fundamental questions of himself, in part through the questions he asks of Sebald: "The past speaks. Will and can Sebald listen? Can he even hear? And if he can hear and listen, what will he say in reply? What will be the tone, the substance, the trajectory of his witness?" (Hansen, p. 127).

It's a stunning piece of writing, and in it one finds hints of David's own longing—to link the work of remembrance to the work he was beginning to envision—doing the ethical inner work as researcher, philosopher, writer, person, that would allow him to act as a moral witness to the daily lives of classroom teachers. Like many qualitative researchers, David's philosophy had always been that we all—students, teachers, cultural "players" of any sort—live our lives somewhat on automatic. He'd always tried to decipher human meanings, to get as close to them as possible as they actually live in people's hearts. But never before had he felt such an inkling of a new method of observation, one based on a pure desire to witness teachers at work and to develop that desire into a humanistic enactment of solidarity. He might be able to offer to the field of education the kind of writing that Sebald had offered to other landscapes of human experience.

He began what he would later call *paying visits to the being of teachers*— by quietly sitting in the corner of their classrooms in New York City, aiming to be as unobtrusive, silent, and invisible as possible as he observed their work. David's line from his essay bears repeating: "Sebald is obsessively concerned not to trespass wrongfully." It was guidance he was now trying to follow.

The people Sebald longed for others to see in their fullness were those who were exiled from their homes and lands because of Hitler. David's longing is more anticipatory, connected to personal, social, and political realities of being a teacher; the personal histories, institutional ethos(es), and hierarchical policies that hold power over teachers' daily work lives. David and Sebald's work connects in its deep recognition of the consequences of dehumanizing individuals under any circumstances and in any ways—by those in power. Like Sebald's imagining of the lives of refugees, David is intent on documenting teachers' professional fullness before their daily truths are lost or hidden away, before something vital is disappeared from the soul of education, hardened and transformed by excessive regulations and standardization of education in the United States.

"I'm still not sure I can say I 'know' what I'm doing here," David emailed me a few months into his work. "Just that it's a doing that feels right—I trust whatever it is (not reducible to 'me') that leads me on" (Hansen, 2014).

In 2017, he completed the essay that describes his work and from which the epigraph to this chapter comes.

"To bear witness to teaching and teachers," David writes in his essay on moral witness, "is to hone one's receptivity to resonant particulars in the school and classroom, a patient, ungrasping approach toward the 'quiet testimony' such particulars express" (Hansen, 2017, p. 11).

"Bearing witness necessitates an ever-deepening attentiveness to what Jan Zwicky calls 'resonant particulars' . . . moments, actions, expressions, and gestures that bring the being of a human being into presence, however fleetingly. Such particulars 'resound with being' (Hansen, 2017, pp. 10–11).

The witness enacts a reflective, critical solidarity with the practice, as mindful as possible of the forces undermining it" (Hansen, 2017, p. 17).

As David's words reveal, his purpose is not to capture that reality in the sense of containing it, *pinning it to a wall*. His aim, in the fullest sense, is to do "right by it" as witness and as writer. David and W. G. Sebald could not care about the people they focus on in exactly the way they do without caring (in exactly the way they do) about finding language that the philosopher Charles Taylor (1989) calls "invocative"—clear, direct, uncluttered. David has always been a language person. But to open himself to his witnessing work, he needed to become more fully aware of more embodied forms of communication—gestures, movement—communication that bypasses verbal language. He worked to develop in himself an openness to the mysteries that live in small details of classroom life, but with a continuous recognition of the necessity of keeping whole human beings in view. Sebald evoked the enormity of leave-taking that marks the lives of refugees, for instance, in his rendering of small goodbyes: "Aunt Fini now stood on the pavement in front of her bungalow, in a dark winter coat too heavy for her, waving a handkerchief after me" (Sebald, 1996, p. 104). To open himself to the hard work of filtering everything through a scrim of potential significance, David burrowed into the paradox of being both fully present and fully absent from his own life, his own "self-ness," opening his five senses to counter the usual self-absorption through which we tend to sift what we see and hear. "I can be a student of Sebald," David wrote me when his moral witness work entered its second year. "And over time, perhaps come to embody at least a meaningful trace of his sensibility of remembrance and make a part of my being the names, faces, scenes, accomplishments of people displaced" (Hansen, 2015).

There is a line sometimes attributed to William James: "Try to be a person upon whom nothing is lost." I think he meant, try to see things as they really are. David Hansen makes this mysterious reach of mind and heart somehow look easy, though of course it is not. He sees his work as an educational researcher and philosopher as an ongoing quest to find new avenues for seeing what is truly so, for *paying visits to being*. As he writes in his essay on moral witness, his own wonder "springs, in part, from the very fact that something called teaching truly does happen or, put differently, happens truly" (Hansen, 2017, p. 15).

I've never met anyone more open to cultivating an attuned compassion toward the world of teaching, attending to its nuance, its ever-changing complexity, its challenge, its beauty, aiming to honor and preserve the ways it happens, truly.

REFERENCES

Hansen, D. T. (2012a). W. G. Sebald and the tasks of ethical and moral remembrance. In C. W. Ruitenberg (Ed.), *Philosophy of education yearbook* (pp. 125–133). Philosophy of Education Society.

Hansen, D. T. (2012b). Notes in Sebald's book. Message to Caroline Heller. July 9. Email.

Hansen, D. T. (2014). Re: your latest. Message to Caroline Heller. February 25. Email.

Hansen, D. T. (2015). Re: your latest. Message to Caroline Heller. July 14. Email.

Hansen, D. T. (2017). Among school teachers: Bearing witness as an orientation in educational inquiry. *Educational Theory*, 67(1), 9–30.

Sebald, W. G. (1996). *The emigrants* (M. Hulse, Trans.). New Directions Books.

Taylor, C. (1989). *Sources of the self: The making of the modern identity*. Harvard University Press.

Afterword

To take seriously is to give sustained attention to something. It is a mark of involvement. Ultimately, it is a sign of respect: respect for the world in which we dwell, and respect for thinking in all its generativity across realms of inquiry, teaching, community life, politics, and more. I am moved to have had things I've written about teaching taken so seriously by the contributors to this volume, including by its able editor, Darryl De Marzio. It is the fulfillment of every scholar's hope, etched into the words they painstakingly assemble for public consideration. I warmly thank these colleagues and friends.

I find the chapters in the volume absorbing. For one thing, they are true to the spirit and the letter of my sense of the call to teach (and I look forward to responding to the contributors' interpretations in detail elsewhere). For another thing, I am fascinated by how the authors take what I've said and point beyond it to the larger, longstanding conversation about teaching that has made it possible for each of us to cultivate what Anna Pagès, in her contribution, calls a "voice." No teacher, and no scholar of teaching, springs de novo on the scene. The moment they walk through "the doorway into education," metaphorically speaking, they immediately encounter and participate in pedagogical traditions that reach back to inaugurating thinkers such as Confucius and Socrates. This lineage is not an unbroken or steadily progressing inheritance. Like actual classroom teaching, the unstoppable conversation on teaching moves through fits and starts, and often commences all over again: sometimes out of dissatisfaction with previous notions of education, sometimes out of a primordial sense of wonder at the very idea of "education"—at the often hard-to-grasp facts of human being and becoming—or sometimes out of a deep urge to rectify problems in culture and society. In this light, every teacher and every scholar of teaching is, in principle, always a beginner: not just because they all start with much to learn, but because each must begin, again and again, to turn to account what they learn in light of their particular circumstances, endeavors, questions, and the like. The mirror to these truths is that the long conversation on teaching itself always begins, again, with each new entrant.

   Perhaps the single most important value in the conversation on teaching is foregrounding the complexity, the challenge, and the significance of teaching, including in the face of skeptics who conflate teaching with the mechanistic transmission of information and skills, and of policymakers and members of the public who reduce teaching to mere job training. Many teachers regard the work as sacred, if not in so many words, in which they point not to particular religious values or beliefs, but rather to the extraordinarily profound meaning and accomplishment people have experienced in the practice. They attest to how both students and they themselves often transform holistically into wiser, more thoughtful, more sensitive human beings, precisely through their educational time together. They also underscore the precariousness and vulnerability in teaching. The price of transformation is suffering, not in the sense of undergoing actual pain (though this can happen in the inevitable aporetic moments in the work), but rather in experiencing what it means to let go of a previous idea or understanding—including what may hitherto have been a valued self-understanding. Without friction, there is no education, only stasis. Teachers know this truth in their bones. It is one of many challenging, but ultimately redeeming, truths of the work that the perennial conversation on teaching keeps in view.

   The conversation is global in nature. This fact illuminates why, at a certain point in my career, I found myself taking up the relation between cosmopolitanism and education. I have had the privilege of traveling to numerous countries and interacting with scholars and teachers from diverse cultural backgrounds. I have met the contributors to this volume in places where they live and work: Indrani Bhattacharjee in Bengaluru where she hosted a conference; Catherine Bell in her classroom and elsewhere in Chicago; Darryl De Marzio in New York City when he was a doctoral student, and in numerous places since then; Ruth Heilbronn and Pádraig Hogan in London and Oxford (though Pádraig works in Dublin); Caroline Heller in Chicago and Boston and points in between; Hansjorg Hohr in Oslo and New York City where he was a visiting professor in the program I direct; Margaret Latta in Okangan, and at more meetings of the American Educational Research Association than I can remember; Anna Pagès in Barcelona, as well as a visit she made to New York City; Shelley Sherman at conferences and in Chicago when she was a doctoral student at my previous institution, the University of Illinois at Chicago (where I composed *The Call to Teach*); and Huajun Zhang in Beijing as well as at numerous conferences.

   Over the course of these encounters, all of them formative and meaningful to me in ways I cannot do justice to here, I finally realized something obvious: Educators constitute a cosmopolitan community. They share countless questions regarding teaching, teacher education, curriculum, assessment, policy, and more. They are mindful of educational ideas and practices developed in contexts quite different from their own. They draw on and infuse these notions into their own work in singular ways, even while dwelling dynamically within educational traditions in which they have grown up. The conversation the contributors have generated in the pages of this book, which relies and builds on the longer-standing conversation touched on previously, brings alive this universal quality. It is a universality based not on agreement about the meaning of teaching, as such, but on the conviction that teaching is real, is humanly important, and is worthy of sustained inquiry, dialogue, and support. The conversation embodies a unity without uniformity.

Where does the idea of teaching as a calling figure into the conversation on teaching? Or, as Darryl De Marzio asks in his introduction: Why use the language of vocation to describe teaching? The call to teach is at once an invitation and a challenge. It invites teachers into a practice that will give back rich, potentially lifelong meaning if they give themselves over to it. This commitment does not mean teachers must describe, in so many words, their work as a calling in order to perform it well. However, they do need to approach and work out the ethical challenge embedded in the call. The challenge is to engage the aesthetic, moral, intellectual, and emotional dimensions embedded in the work, which the contributors to this volume flesh out in multicolored fashion. The idea of teaching as a calling intensifies the significance of a many-sided question that every teacher confronts in one way or another, and does so continuously as long as they remain in the practice: What is the teacher's *relation* with students, curriculum, the school, society, and their own self? As countless dedicated teachers have attested, it takes considerable time to develop this relation, with students and curriculum at the "everyday center" of things, but ramifying into the other domains mentioned. In a recent, long-term project I undertook with a group of New York City public school teachers, one of the participants, a 10-year veteran of middle school teaching, shared the following self-disclosure:

> I thought it'd be a lot easier, the teaching. . . . But I've been disabused again and again of the idea that teaching is easy. I was definitely a little bit egotistical and arrogant entering my first teaching job, thinking: "I'm a smart guy, I can do this." . . . But the development of the teaching craft and teaching instincts—I was not a good teacher until working at this school [where he was entering his third year, after working for seven years in another school]. I feel like I've just continued to grow . . . I read the idea "Oh, you can get a good teacher with a lot of support in one year." But if you think about "good" as having to do with a person developing into his or her capabilities and capacities, then you absolutely don't get a "good" teacher [that quickly]. (Recorded interview)

The dedication I have witnessed time and again in teachers in schools mirrors the commitment to deep educational values the contributors to this book express. To revive the language of calling means, among other things, attending to the lives of teachers, newcomers and veterans alike, in the spirit of this commitment. Teacher educators, researchers on teaching, policymakers, and others whose actions affect teachers do not have to look outside the call to teach for guidance, just as they do not need to act as if there is no ongoing conversation about the practice. As this book demonstrates, the conversation is always happening. I encourage readers to listen in and participate. The continued life and well-being of teaching depend on it.

I am looking again now at the cover of this book of essays that Darryl De Marzio has graciously and masterfully orchestrated. The cover features Winslow Homer's painting (completed in 1870) entitled *The Schoolmistress*. There is nothing romantic, or cynical or jaded, about the painter's rendering. He approaches the task in a sober, respectful manner: He takes his client with the utmost seriousness. Her expression conveys her considerable experience in the classroom. She is neither excited nor anxious. She is not at ease, standing there in the artist's studio, but also not aloof or cold. She looks straight ahead. Perhaps she sees in her mind's eye the expected and unexpected happenings she will encounter once she reaches her classroom. But she does look ahead; she goes to meet the work. I imagine the painter feeling at times that she is looking right through him. She has more important things to do, and she is readying herself.

About the Contributors

Catharine (Catie) Bell teaches high school English at the University of Chicago Laboratory Schools where, with her students and colleagues, she explores connections between literature and moral philosophy. She received her PhD from the University of Chicago's Department of Education applying John Dewey's ideas about art to teaching 8th-grade humanities. She remains grateful to the "Moral Life of Schools" project for helping her find words to describe her interests.

Indrani Bhattacharjee is assistant professor of philosophy of education at Azim Premji University, Bangalore. She is currently engaged in writing a book on Tagore's philosophical thought circa 1908–1916.

Darryl M. De Marzio (Editor) is professor of foundations of education at the University of Scranton. He received his PhD in philosophy and education from Teachers College, Columbia University, writing his dissertation under the supervision of David Hansen. His research interests include the ethics of teaching, philosophy and childhood, and the history of educational ideas.

David T. Hansen is the John L. and Sue Ann Weinberg Professor in the Historical and Philosophical Foundations of Education at Teachers College, Columbia University, where he also serves as director of the Program in Philosophy and Education. Hansen has written widely on the work of teachers, including in books such as *The Call to Teach* (1995), *Exploring the Moral Heart of Teaching* (2001), and *The Teacher and the World* (2011). Before taking up his present position, Hansen was director for 10 years of the secondary teacher education program at the University of Illinois at Chicago. He is a past-president of the John Dewey Society and of the Philosophy of Education Society, and is a fellow of the American Educational Research Association.

Ruth Heilbronn researches and lectures at UCL Institute of Education, where she has led various teams engaged in teacher education. She previously taught in inner London secondary schools and worked as an LEA advisor. She has written on the epistemology of practice, mentoring, practical judgment, and ethical teacher education. John Dewey has figured largely in her work as an editor of several collections and organizer of conferences. She is an executive member of the Philosophy of Education Society of Great Britain.

Caroline Heller is professor and director of the PhD Program in Educational Studies, Interdisciplinary Specialization, Lesley University, in Cambridge, Massachusetts. She is the author of *Until We Are Strong Together* (Teachers College Press, 1997) and *Reading Claudius: A Memoir in Two Parts* (Dial Press, Random House, 2015).

Pádraig Hogan is an emeritus of the National University of Ireland Maynooth. He has a keen research interest in the quality of educational experience and in what makes learning environments conducive to fruitful learning. Prior to retirement, he led the research and development program "Teaching and Learning for the 21st Century" (TL21), an action research initiative with over 70 secondary schools that continues to grow yearly. His books include *The Custody and Courtship of Experience: Western Education in Philosophical Perspective* (1995); *The New Significance of Learning: Imagination's Heartwork* (2010); and *Towards a Better Future: A Review of the Irish School System* (coauthored with J. Coolahan, S. Drudy, Á. Hyland, and S. McGuinness, 2017).

Hansjörg Hohr is a retired professor in philosophy of education at the University of Oslo and Trondheim (Norway). Previously, he worked for many years in teacher education at colleges in Tromsø and Trondheim. He has published extensively on aesthetic education.

Margaret Macintyre Latta is a professor and director of the Okanagan School of Education, Faculty of Education, University of British Columbia, Canada. Her scholarship emphasizes the primacy of educators in the lives of their students toward learning/learner growth and well-being. Alongside K–16 educators, school districts, and community sites, she seeks ways to engage students (and others) in cocurricular-making, as integral within learning of all kinds. **Elizabeth Saville** is an accomplished educator of 22 years with particular expertise in STEM education and experiential learning, who has recently returned to doctoral studies in education. **Lisa Marques** and **Katie Wihak** are awesome educators, passionately committed to ongoing professional growth, invested in love of learning for learning's sake.

Anna Pagès is a senior researcher in philosophy of education at Blanquerna-Faculty of Education, Ramon Llull University in Barcelona (Spain). Her field of study includes hermeneutics and education, tradition from a pedagogical perspective, feminist philosophy and the philosophical background of the early 20th-century progressive school movement. She is the author of

At the Edge of the Past (2005), *On Oblivion* (2012), and *Dinner with Diotime: A Philosophy of the Feminine* (2017).

Shelley Sherman is associate professor of education emerita at Lake Forest College. She is the author of *Teacher Preparation as an Inspirational Practice: Building Capacities for Responsiveness* (2013), for which she received the award for Exemplary Research in Teaching and Teacher Education from the American Educational Research Association in 2015.

Huajun Zhang is associate professor at the Institute of Teacher Education Research, Faculty of Education, Beijing Normal University. Her primary research interest is in the philosophy of teaching and teacher education.

Index